EMOTIONAL LIBERATION
LIFE BEYOND TRIGGERS AND TRAUMA

A Guide to Your
Psychological Immune System

By GuruMeher Khalsa

atmosphere press

Praise for GuruMeher Khalsa's
Emotional Liberation

Better than twenty years of therapy!

    – Lisa Davidowitz, Marketing Consultant

I was so surprised at the changes that came from the power of validating my feelings. I now have the tools to heal myself for a lifetime of emotional well-being.

    – Bruce Jackson, Trauma Survivor

In his groundbreaking work, GuruMeher Khalsa reveals the pivotal role difficult emotions serve in healing and offers a step-by-step method for releasing trauma.

    – Becca Williams, RDN, emotional wellness educator

This book elucidates practical therapeutic strategies that facilitate a positive relationship with one's emotional characteristic, history, and patterns of behavior to bring about an elevated emotional maturity, intelligence and a personal transformation.

    – Sat Bir S. Khalsa, Ph.D., Asst. Professor of Medicine,
    Harvard Medical School

Having followed GuruMeher's work for the past 40 years, it is with great pleasure I endorse his new book. *Emotional Liberation* gives great hope for this world by elevating us to live a more loving and nurturing life. Thank you, GuruMeher!

    – Gurmukh Kaur, Legacy Yoga Teacher

This work with grief has got me feeling joy. I'm excited about life again.

    – Lisa Botts, Entrepreneur

GuruMeher's work has done wonders for me and so many of my clients who suffer from trauma-based shame and lack of self-love.

– Annette D, Counselor

I've learned from this work that emotions are messages that are meant to help us get to a state of peace. I can now use every painful emotion constructively. When I recognize and allow them, go into my heart and listen, something transformative happens. It never fails.

– Clifford Bochner, MD

I now see how my past trauma was at the core of everything that was holding me back. I pushed through life so hard, even success was painful. Emotional Liberation has helped me turn my numbed shame into self-love.

– Atma Nilsson, Psychiatric Nurse

GuruMeher provides holistic guidance for listening to and responding to our most challenging feelings. He compassionately weaves science and spirituality together to help transform emotional energy into evolutionary wisdom.

– Susan Bernstein, PhD (Somatic Psychology)

In this book, GuruMeher offers a clear pathway to emotional freedom. You will learn how to transform trauma and reactivity into purpose and possibility. You will be empowered to identify patterns or false beliefs and reprogram your behavior for a life of success.

– Kia Miller, founder of Radiant Body Yoga

Also by GuruMeher Khalsa:

Senses of the Soul: Emotional Therapy
for Strength, Healing & Guidance

Our life is not our own; it comes as a gift through many hands and hearts. Thank you Nels Arnold, Steve Sigur, Clelle Kinney, Siri Atma Kaur, Siri Gian, Lisa Davidowitz, Becca Williams and the countless teachers in my family, students and clients, many of whose stories are shared here.

Contents

An Invitation to Healthcare Professionals

As a yoga therapist, I have spent four decades practicing, teaching and applying mindfulness techniques to nurture self-inquiry and self-healing among thousands of students and clients.

The qualitative data I have gathered support a remarkable discovery that painful emotions are integral to a natural system of psychological healing and keys to mental/emotional well-being. I have learned to trust feelings to reliably show me what the client needs to feel better. Far better than that, clients can do this for themselves: we can teach them to follow emotions to their own solutions. It is my hope that teachers and healthcare professionals will do this self-healing work with emotions to benefit personally and, in turn, use it to augment their ability to help others. In this way, we can help to raise the standard of human happiness and well-being.

In this work, we approach trauma as being common to the human condition, while recognizing that it occurs on a broad spectrum. My work has been primarily with those suffering from repetitive, developmental and intergenerational forms of trauma. Those of you working with acute and complex trauma will find great help from Emotional Liberation using your specialized trauma-sensitive training. I invite you to adapt this work in your practice to discover its effectiveness. To best help others—and not be negatively affected while doing our work—we healers must befriend and work skillfully with our own emotions.

Due to our widespread personal and cultural mis-understanding that emotions are themselves a problem, you and your clients may be hesitant to dive into them. You will find that there is built-in safety to this work in that the client/patient does the work and therefore retains control. You, equipped with the guidance of this book, can serve to assist their process of self-therapy. Since a client/patient will not venture far into voluntarily recalling an emotional experience in which they don't feel safe, the process is self-regulating.

Your job is to be the trusted guide—much as a skilled scuba dive-master can safely introduce the novice diver to the ocean's beauty. Like that dive-master, your assignment is first to explore your own emotional depths and learn to navigate them safely. You must be able to understand and work with your emotions. This cannot be accomplished by reading alone, but by the direct, personal experience. "Doing the work" enables you to develop trust in natural emotional responses, emotions' purpose and their ability to bring relief and healing.

General Protocol for Emotions

Here is a brief summary of a simple process I use with exceptional results in most every session to help clients be the source of their own answers and healing. In various forms, it is used in the exercises throughout this book, which is designed to facilitate self-therapy by the reader. Self-awareness and healing can be greatly accelerated when these techniques are taught and assisted by a trained practitioner. (Readers, you may benefit from seeking such support.) Therapists use verbal cues to guide the client through each stage in conjunction with any body-centered techniques with which they are familiar. The client may succeed with each step in one session, or it may take successive sessions to access these states and answers.

1. Create stillness
2. Create safety
3. Create clarity
4. Create internal awareness

5. Activate emotion by inviting memories
6. Acclimate to the emotion
7. Encourage equilibrium and "comfort" with the feelings
8. Communicate with the emotion—may be verbal, mental, visual, wordlessly intuitive
9. Ask for the source of the emotion
10. Ask for solution
11. Visualize action
12. Go back often for more information throughout a session or in successive sessions
13. Teach the client to do this process themselves as they feel safe to do so

If you would like further training to facilitate this work, see https://sensesofthesoul.com/sos-facilitator/

What Is Emotional Liberation?

This book is about taking back control of the emotions and situations that control you; to use strong emotions as medicine rather than poison. It is a self-initiated, hands-on approach to mental and emotional wellness. It is a journey on which you will recognize how painful experiences have separated you from your best self and that you have the inborn ability to learn and grow stronger from those challenges. You will find, as I have, that we were misinformed about the role and value of our emotions. You will re-acquire the ability to use emotions that arise when you are upset to heal the past, prevent further harm and bring peace.

A System of Self-Therapy

We have all been hurt, which means we're all recovering from something. It might be what your father did to you decades ago, what your mother didn't do, or that joke your friend made about you yesterday; you still feel hurt and angry today. Painful experiences tear away pieces of us: parts of our innocence, bits of confidence, chunks of peace, years of happiness. But we are built to recover, to learn from pain and become stronger. Self-healing is an inborn ability; it is your birthright.

I have spent the last forty years studying, practicing and teaching self-awareness using meditative practices combined with modern psychology. The prevailing view of emotions by meditative practices has been that they are a weakness and personal failing and a medical disorder to be treated and cured by modern psychology; in both instances, emotions are seen as something to overcome. In my personal life and professional experience as a yoga therapist, neither approach works. You will find, as I have, the precious value of your feelings.

Imagine that whenever you "feel bad," you would always know why you feel that way, what you need, then do that to feel better. You could navigate life by solving problems, recovering quickly and spending more time being happy. You do have this ability, ready and waiting to be discovered and used. Whatever you may have been struggling and wrestling with for however long, you can now raise the quality of your mental/emotional health. It takes time and training, as does any talent or skillset, but if you will dedicate yourself to "working out" in the gym of your inner world of thoughts and feelings, you will feel better. Emotional Liberation is available to everyone willing to do the work.

How It Works

Here is a recent example of one woman's discovery of her self-healing abilities. Alice sat with me for a session, curious how Emotional Liberation might add to her work as a psychologist to better help people. When I asked how I might help her, she didn't have any particular issues to talk about. Moreover, she added that she didn't usually have much emotion and made it clear that she certainly did not want to feel or deal with any in this session.

After a bit of discussion, I invited her to close her eyes, breathe slowly and pay attention to her body and how she felt. When she was calm and secure, I began to ask her questions about what she was feeling. Before long, she shared a big problem with her mother that had been troubling her since she was a child. She cried. I invited her to stay present with me and her breath while allowing herself to feel the uncomfortable feelings of sadness without trying to stop them. Slowly she calmed and became quiet as I asked her what the sadness showed her. She spoke confidently about what was upsetting her, what she needed to know and do to resolve her problem. I simply wrote down her exact words. Twenty minutes had passed since she closed her eyes.

As she opened her eyes, she looked at me and said, *"That was amazing. How did you do that?"* I told her that I have studied how emotions work and had simply helped her to work with them. Her willingness to tap into her feelings without becoming emotionally activated led her to understand her situation and see a way out. She was now quite sure what she needed to do and felt so much better, encouraged and hopeful. Her assignment now was to return home and act on the realizations that had become apparent to her.

Stories of self-realization and inner guidance like this come out of nearly every therapy session I give. These results don't depend on my skills as a therapist; I assist the client in discovering the answers that are within them. How? First, by facilitating their self-awareness with simple mindfulness practices, then by using their increased clarity to work with their feelings. Emotions are part of the human Psychological Immune System which detects disruptions to our well-being. Your feelings are vital resources to be used to handle life's challenges.

Trends in Emotional Health

In the last century, the knowledge of physical health discovered by science and "alternative" modalities significantly advanced the average person's access to longevity and fitness. We are healthier but not happier. Psychological disorders are said to be epidemic and stress has become the primary source of physical illness and death.

This makes mental/emotional health our next challenge. This century will bring a quantum leap in the awareness and tools to manage our inner worlds of thought and feeling to achieve advanced levels of well-being and happiness.

Another phenomenon is driving this trend; the pace of life is accelerating, so we are being forced—or invited—to learn more quickly. For that, we need greater awareness and sensitivity to see what is happening, not just here and now but below the surface of things and before they happen so we can prepare rather than get hit. Like it or not, you and everyone around you is becoming more sensitive; you feel more and more strongly. That causes stress and overwhelm, mania and depression and their reactions of rage, conflict and self-harm.

A third significant change underway is the democratization of power. Everyone can now access cutting edge information and technology that was once controlled by the few in power. Psychology, like physical health, has been a mystery and healing was the work of only the experts. Many people find practical help outside the mainstream channels of medicine; you may be one of them. As brain and behavior become better understood, we can effectively work with ourselves to manage mind, mood and the behaviors that determine our quality of life. To need help with mental health is no longer a stigma; we more openly discuss and deal with our troubles. When did you first hear the terms trauma, triggers, activation, or recovery? As these terms and concepts come into our vocabulary, they mark advancing awareness and skills we are all developing.

Help Yourself

You are part of these trends leading humanity out of the psychological dark ages. We are all recovering from something and need to manage the effects of it. And who can know better than you what is wrong and what to do about it? Because we have all the information about our needs and unique solutions inside, who is in a better position to help you? "Self-help" will no longer be seen as inferior to the techniques and opinions of professionals; every individual has the privilege and power to help themselves. Knowledge of and for the self shall come from the self. The job of therapists, counselors and healers will increasingly be to teach us how to use our self-healing system.

Emotional Liberation—A Journey and a Destination

Emotional Liberation is not freedom from emotions. We begin by recasting their very qualities and functions: "negative" emotions ("bad" feelings) are protective and "positive" emotions ("good" feelings) are thriving and flourishing. Each in its time and place is as important and essential as your heartbeat. You cannot rid yourself of feelings, nor would you want to, for they are the carriers of love and peace as well. Being emotionally liberated is to live fully with your feelings, working intelligently to let them serve you, to enjoy the highs and gracefully move through the low points in life. When emotionally liberated, you keep your cool when others are losing theirs. When emotionally agile, you can adequately feel strong emotions without being stuck in them as they help you deal with the situations that provoke them. When emotionally skillful, you understand what others are feeling and can help them rather than react.

Emotions, as a path to that freedom, are undoubtedly a double-edged sword. They can either bind us to a painful past or be the impetus to grow past it. Anger can make us lose control or give us the power to take control. Instead of permanent residents in our bodies and remnants of our history, emotions can heal us from the traumas that muddy our past, haunt the present and cloud the future. The word trauma describes both an adverse experience as well as the ongoing psychological conditions we live in as a result. Similarly, emotional liberation is first a process of mindfully using emotions for recovery from everyday upsets and past harms. Emotional liberation is also a state of being and way of living free to feel life fully and move smoothly through pleasure and pain.

You can learn to work with your emotions to recover from traumatic events and their ensuing reactive behaviors so that, eventually, nothing can disturb your inner peace. To act from a stable center, rather than reacting to situations, to be free of traumas and triggers. Emotional Liberation is to safely feel emotions as they naturally arise and to utilize them to move through all challenges and reach peace.

The core of Emotional Liberation work is to develop this simple ability. Whenever you feel bad, you:

1. Know what you are feeling
2. Know why you are feeling it
3. Know what you need to feel better
4. Act on this knowledge until you feel better

I encourage you to set a goal to achieve this level of self-understanding and self-management. Then you can help your children, parents, patients and clients to do the same. Help me hold a vision that with this skillset, you and all of humanity can live in peace.

Imagine with me that having this capability is standard human capacity. Doesn't it seem self-evident that we would all possess the self-awareness and self-control to take care of ourselves this well? Isn't it rather primitive, sad and even tragic that this ability goes mostly unused in the present civilization we consider advanced?

Now imagine every person using their ability to self-soothe after every wound, to take care of their needs and live with contentment. Imagine decision-makers, power-holders and leaders who control and affect laws and others' lives with this level of emotional processing. Imagine you and your closest loved ones moving quickly and satisfyingly through the issues that arise. In this vision, I see a healthy world; it is well within your personal power and reach.

Now is the time to stop looking outside yourself for
salvation and begin looking to yourself for wisdom and help,
to know yourself and get what you need to be safe and happy.
Reclaim the inner guidance that your caregivers failed to
encourage—or worse—beat out of you due to their pain. This
book will give you information and tools to heal old wounds,
learn and grow from trauma and change old trauma-created
reactive patterns. We can recover our natural ability to
recover. Here is an outline of the process.

A Model for Self-Therapy

When you go to a doctor for treatment, she begins by
identifying your symptoms: your problem and pain. She uses
her knowledge of how the body works to locate the source,
what is not working and what caused your good health to go
awry. She then prescribes a treatment, designed to help the
body return to health. You will follow these same steps to your
emotional health: self-examination leading to understanding
the cause and applying known remedies to correct what is
ailing you.

Examination—Do I Know What Is Happening?

Each life can take care of itself. Who could know you better
than yourself? We are born with self-awareness but quickly
become focused on the five senses, directed outward to get
what we need. Beyond meeting basic physical needs, keeping
yourself happy requires knowing yourself very well. The
equipment you have to do so includes:
- The ability to tune in to bodily sensations—somatic
   experiencing
- The ability to observe your thoughts—meta-cognition

- The ability to feel your feelings—emotional sensitivity
- The accurate instincts of your reptilian brain—automatic reactions
- The powerfully motivating emotions of your mammalian brain—it is hardwired
- The understanding and rational choice from your analytical brain—powerful but not always under our control
- And the agency or will to be in charge and coordinate these often-conflicted parts of the self.

The many techniques of meditation are all designed to develop self-awareness. They range from ancient yogic practices to recent techniques developed through brain scanning research. I will use the term and simple techniques popularly known as "mindfulness." The goal is to improve the ability to focus one's attention at will and as needed, rather than having the mind busy, scattered and unable to perceive clearly, to be "present" to what is here and now.

Using your self-awareness faculties, start by examining the "symptoms." In the next chapter, you will identify the frequent uncomfortable thoughts and feelings, dysfunctional behaviors and unwanted situations in your life. They show up again and again so you can see them, get sick of and want to change them. The repetition of your patterns can make them invisible; you learn to live with them—perhaps miserably. But by focusing your attention on them and identifying the many elements of these automatic reactions, the mystery of why you act counter to your interests begins to become apparent. And from that comes the ability to choose and to change.

As awareness of yourself and your situations increases, you begin to gain control over misery-making subconscious behaviors and make conscious decisions that promote your well-being. Identifying your patterns and triggers is the first step. Whether you already know yours or they take some time to recognize, it will be of great value to go through the self-analysis process in Chapter 1.

Diagnosis—Do I Understanding the Problem?

Mental distress and emotional turmoil are symptoms we feel, but they do not of themselves solve a problem any more than does the pain of an infected tooth. An understanding of cause and treatment is needed and is made easier with some system of how things work. A psychiatrist looks at your symptoms, then goes to the DSM for an established understanding to give the condition a name and a recommended treatment. Emotions are symptoms present in every problem. Knowing that they are the treatment, their purpose and how they achieve it to solve the problem is a "DSM," a highly evolved natural system of psychological self-healing. Chapters 5 through 11 invite you to discover it for yourself. (*The Diagnostic and Statistical Manual of Mental Disorders*—DSM—is an authoritative volume that defines and classifies mental disorders to improve diagnoses, treatment and research, developed over many years by experts in all aspects of mental health.)

Treatment—What is Needed?

What makes humans tick is not a great mystery, but changing circumstances, random events and our individual and ever-present desires create complications. Here again, self-awareness is the way to know what you need to get through personal dysfunction and move on to something better. You always know what to do and can reawaken that ability. You have been doing self-therapy all your life. You may not remember your early desperate need to be warm and fed as a newborn, but your ongoing adjustment to life on Earth was not easy and it's been challenging even in the best of cases. Many of us dealt with much worse situations. Through

14

it all, we have been adapting and evolving to meet these situations in attempts—sometimes successful and other times not—to at least survive and at best to be happy. It has been a slow learning process throughout history.

Get Packing

Today, challenge and change are too swift and constant. We can no longer afford to repeat the unconscious patterns we inherit, to suffer many broken relationships to learn how to connect. We are experiencing an evolutionary pressure to learn from every pain how to avoid pain, from every fall how to rise, from every wound how we can heal ourselves. Go beyond reading this book to advance your self-empowered journey of healing, growth and change. Here are a few things to take along on your trip.

- Safety First—Self-therapy is self-regulated; you are in control. Go only as deep, fast, or far as you feel you can handle.
- Take Responsibility—Yes, people did things to you, it's your job to take care of yourself now.
- Empower Yourself—Unwanted things aren't just happening to you; you create your life.
- Experience is the Teacher—Learn from past pain how to avoid it. Learn from peace what works.
- Get Guidance and Support—Moving from "needing help" to "self-help" includes experienced help from others.
- Accept and Allow—Face ugliness until you no longer fear it; that is the hero's path.

Emotions are here to help you; let them! The same feelings that come when you are hurt are trying to protect and heal. Your primitive fight, flight and freeze reactions that worked for our jungle ancestors need you to guide them to serve modern needs. Your brain's "executive" decision-making function can blend instinctual urge with sophisticated calculation to alchemically produce wisdom, answers and elevated action.

This book offers the theory and practice to heal yourself from all types of psychological wounds.

Imagine every human using their ability to detect and correct their upsets. We'd still have conflicts as neighbors and nations, but we'd have the tools to know what we are fighting about and begin addressing and solving our internal issues first and the real problems with each other.

Five Principles of Emotional Liberation

Emotional Liberation is both the process of utilizing emotions for psychological self-healing and the experience of freedom from trauma's adverse effects. Here are five fundamental features of this therapeutic approach to psychological healing.

1—We All Have Patterns (Chapter 1)

These are learned emotional reactions to certain stimuli—our triggers—in which we lose conscious control and react in ways that work against our best interests. You will define yours in Chapter 1 and begin to upgrade them with responses that make things better rather than worse.

2—We Have All Suffered Trauma (Chapter 2)

To varying degrees of intensity, everyone has been hit by life events. These are the source of our patterns. Compassionate understanding of our traumas and transforming them into positive change-makers is the work of Chapter 2.

3—We Are Built for Recovery (Chapter 3)

Through the existential hardship of life, we evolved an inborn system of psychological self-healing. Hard knocks create blocks but also stimulate growth. Just as life events have a full mind/body/emotional impact, we must bring all our faculties into the healing process; recovery is experiential. Self-Therapy, using what you know about yourself and can do for yourself, is the future of therapy. Discovering and utilizing it is our goal. In Chapter 3, we will pick up the tools that assist self-awareness, which is the basis of self-therapy.

4—Emotions Are Keys to Recovery (Chapter 4)

Emotions have been misunderstood and misused, but are essential to our natural healing abilities. You have a psychological immune system that uses feelings to detect and protect you from invasions of well-being. Chapter 4 will reintroduce you to your emotions as medicine to begin a new working relationship with them.

5—Emotions Are a Complete Therapeutic System (Chapters 5-11)

Once we begin to be more comfortable with troubling emotions in general, we find that each one has very a specific purpose. Just as various antibodies are pathogen-specific. Anger, for example, is sent out to neutralize particular types of harm in your life. Emotions' completely systematic behavior gives a most effective ability to diagnose and treat their cause. Chapters 5 through 11 are a hands-on guide to decoding and skillfully using this innate system for yourself and others.

Part One:
Of Wounds and Recovery

Chapter 1

Triggers and Patterns:
Everyday Issues and Polite Insanity

We Are Walking Wounded

Most of us are "functional;" we can hide our pain and are seen as normal. But behind that mask lives the wounded self. Under stress, she comes out and takes over like the Incredible Hulk. When polite Bruce Banner gets angry, he loses control, becomes a big green monster and when he calms down, awakens to see the destruction he created but hardly remembers. Emotion takes over. How does your "losing it" story go? Why do you react that way? Is there any way to better manage your feelings? I want you to identify and understand the habitual emotional reactions that trouble you and replace them with at-choice behaviors that lead to happiness.

A pattern is a behavioral stimulus-and-response sequence that recurs over and over again. It includes the troubling thoughts we dislike but can't stop, the heavy emotions that feel bad and take over and the unproductive or destructive behaviors we can't control. The thing that activates a pattern is called a trigger. Triggers initiate automatic reactions in which we lose control of our words and actions. We can use these triggers as clues to better understand what is happening inside ourselves and address it. Here we will explore how patterns and triggers work and how to be free from them.

Why do we all have them? They are an ingenious but outdated survival mechanism. In our usual efforts to get what

21

we need, we have been denied, disappointed, shocked and hurt: in a word, wounded. Early in the evolution of species, animals developed an automatic response to adverse experiences designed to avoid further harm of a similar nature. The memories of injury are stored in a database that is subconscious, meaning that they are out of your control and you may not remember them.

Triggers

Even in good times, your mind seeks anything that might put you in a position to be hurt again. It compares the details of any current situation that make you uncomfortable and feel threatening to the earlier case. You develop hyper-sensitivity and automatic responses to specific cues from the past experience. The very presence of the one who hurt you; anyone who looks or acts like them; particular words, tone, or volume of someone who used those same sounds in a fight; the sound of an explosion or a mere passing memory in an otherwise quiet moment. If there is sufficient similarity between the current cues and any stored in your subconscious "databank of harmful things," the current situation is deemed dangerous. The "trigger" is "pulled," and an explosion of defensive reactions follows, starting with the same emotions you felt at the first event. A trigger is a cue that activates your defense mechanisms.

Patterns

As the defender of your safety, the subconscious mind is powerful, but it is not very smart. It can't tell the difference between then and now, between your father and your boyfriend. Nor does it realize you are no longer 3, 6, or 18 but an adult with greater strength, wisdom and skills—and therefore more effective options to deal with the situation—than you had when that earlier incident occurred. When this protective response is "triggered," the consciousness and untrained reactions of that younger "you" take control. You lose access to all the intelligence, experience and options you have gathered through the intervening years. You revert to a much less effective person, may feel defenseless and unable to speak or run away from a relationship you want to build. When emotionally activated, you call on the responses you clung to for survival long ago. The outmoded and ineffective ways you automatically react when triggered are called your patterns.

Imagine your former 8-year-old self in a fight with your current spouse, or your 12-year-old self, receiving criticism from your boss; it looks a lot like that. When your mother says those same hurtful things now that she said back when you were young, you feel just as small and rejected despite who you are now. You look all grown up, but when triggered, the earlier scared child still locked in subconscious memory is arguing with your partner's hurt and angry child. Not much gets worked out between those two ghosts! Once either of you is upset, you will react defensively and likely trigger the other person. Then your wounded self is attacking and defending itself from their wounded self. You and the person you love and respect have both left the building.

Sadly, history is written by adults acting out their wounded stories with each other. Our patterns are primitive survival-based responses from deep within our brain and evolutionary history that are the product of our past and most impactfully from trauma. We can be better than the ancient animal in survival mode that takes over when we feel challenged. How to update our options under adverse situations and become a responsive human rather than a reactive animal? Just as finding the cure for disease starts with observing the symptoms, an essential step in resolving one's traumas is to understand their effects on our behavior clearly.

A pattern is something that repeats itself over and over again. That gives us many chances to see it. Repetition is how we learn; we do a thing over and over to know and then master any skill. A detective has seen so much crime they can solve a case with clues that fit a pattern. Just so, the recurrence of our behavioral patterns helps us to see and then understand them. We repeat our dysfunctional patterns until we learn from, outgrow and replace them with at-choice behaviors. Think of increased happiness as nature's reward for lessons you have learned.

Envision Your Trigger-Free Future

Unpleasant things happened that you have forgotten or avoid but resurface to cause trouble. I want you to dig in, root them out and be free. There is a clear and verifiable way to do so. Set a personal goal to be trigger free. It means you will consciously respond, rather than react emotionally. Unconscious actions do not thwart your intentions. You keep your cool when others are stressing. It doesn't mean you won't feel yourself and the world fully. It means your past, other people, passing thoughts and desires won't send you off the rails and out of control. Feelings will serve your purpose. That nothing can disturb one's inner peace is, unfortunately, a rare thing. If you want to go for it, start now to hold a vision of your non-reactive self. Let it motivate the work that follows.

How long will it take to achieve this state? That depends on your starting point. The degree of trauma, current situation, stress load, physical health, focus and effort invested are factors, but all your efforts will improve outcomes. Let's hold a broader vision for all people to be someday trigger-free: mothers, fathers, friends and leaders. It begins with you, to prove and model for others that it can be done.

I'll Show You Mine

I'll share with you a personal pattern from which I am now (quite nearly) trigger free. As you enjoy the "polite insanity" of my reactions, let them prompt awareness of yours, some of which may have much heavier outcomes. I will then invite you to examine and overcome one of your patterns. This pattern occurs when my wife and I are going somewhere in the car together and I am driving. We are enjoying the day and each other, pleasantly anticipating the destination. But it all changes in an instant when she gives me directions: "Turn right here," or, "There's a stop sign," or if she is startled by brake lights in front of us, or recoils when a large truck is close in the next lane. I instantly become irritated and mad about it. I say, "I know!" "I see it," or even ridicule her for being afraid. Or I may say nothing, but either way I then get quiet; I sulk. She senses the shift in my mood and neither of us speaks for a long, somber while. Ten minutes, the rest of the trip, or the rest of the day may pass before positive feelings return.

This pattern did not exist early in our relationship and it became more intense with years of repetition. Not a big thing, but a simple, everyday pattern like this will spoil any good relationship as it repeats and builds intensity over time. Escalating patterns underlie the too-frequent decline and dissolution in intimate relationships, friendships and business partnerships and explain why the majority of abuse and murder happens within close relationships. Earlier, the same relationships were positive and nurturing, but the reactions intensify and build resentment as frustration and hurt accumulate.

Happily, it didn't come to that for us; we are happily married for many decades and this particular pattern is (just about) gone. Why did I take these cues-become-triggers as attacks and react defensively and angrily? Instead, why didn't I appreciate her assistance and navigation directions? Why don't I respond to her anxiety by driving in a way that puts her at ease? I will get to the "why" —it took time for me to discover it—but first, we'll use my example to see how an unconscious pattern can be revealed, analyzed and disarmed from doing further harm.

The Pattern Formula and Breakdown

For simplicity, distill this complex pattern into a formula (no math skills required).

$X + Y = Z$; Where X is the trigger; Y is an emotion that is activated; Z is the reaction.

As in, everything is fine, but when _____, I feel _____ and then I _____.

Mine: When told what to do, I feel angry and ashamed and then I verbally attack and defend.

This describes the essence, but there is so much more to know about myself before I can change. A recurring pattern is a rapid cascade of automatic reactions. By dissecting it into the ten factors below, each step becomes a point of intervention and recovery. After reading my before-and-after descriptions, you will be invited to analyze a pattern of your own. You may want to begin now by creating your own Reactions Worksheet using the section headings in bold below and summarized afterward (or download a copy at www.emotional-liberation.com/resources) and begin filling it in as you go through this section.

The Pattern

Old: When my wife directs or reacts to my driving, I get irritated (feel hurt and angry) and become sarcastic, make her wrong, want her to stop making comments, or go silent.

New: When my wife advises or reacts to my driving—I feel supported and loved and want to do what I can to help her be more relaxed. This is an intention, a goal, an imagining of my future un-triggered state, which is the first step toward creating it.

My Pattern Name

Old: Mad Advice. This name summarizes and is easily remembered when I find myself in the middle of it.

New: Accepting Tips. Accepting my faults, mistakes and my competence are vital to healing the wounds beneath this pattern. This name identifies how I want to be: open to receiving feedback and help.

1: All is Well—The Calm before the Storm

Old: I am driving, enjoying the day with my wife. I feel good, have positive thoughts and engage with her effortlessly. We are in Dynamic Equilibrium.

New: My goal is to sustain this positive state more continuously, come what may. My larger intention is that we both steer through life, helping each other to be safe and happy.

2: The Trigger—This Initiates the Sequence that Follows

Old: She gives directions, a correction, a warning, or reacts physically to traffic.

New: I can ask her not to give me directions unless I ask for or agree to accept input. I can ask her to drive, so she has control of her safety and route. These avoid the trigger and reduce stress, a first step. But I want more, to heal the wound beneath. Realization and communication bring some relief, get us both trying new things: laughing about it, using words and tones that don't carry disdain, agreeing that when I am the driver she is the navigator so we have roles and work together.

3: The Emotions—What I Feel

Old: irritation; frustration; anger (that she is criticizing me); shame, not-good-enough-ness (that she thinks I don't know/can't do); despondency (that it will never change); fear (that I will be wrong, have an accident, get lost).

New: Emotional reactions are precognitive—we are in them before we "know" it. But when I imagine feeling love, happiness, self-respect, gratitude in this situation I create new neural pathways that can someday be accessed in that moment. (Later we will see that these feelings are the same that arose in earlier situations that formed this pattern.)

4: The Thoughts—Familiar Voices in My Head

Old: "I totally saw that. I know where we are going and what I am doing. She doesn't trust me, thinks I'm stupid. She is so uptight, why can't she relax and trust me? I am a better driver than she is. She always does this; I am sick of it. I should just let her drive, but she isn't a good driver."

New: Later when I am over it and calm, I can match each of my habitual thoughts with a better-feeling, more positive and more truthful one. "Yes, I saw that and am doing fine, she is just nicely helping. It's nice that she cares and wants to help. I could relax and let her navigate for me. Am I driving in a way that makes her feel unsafe and am I willing to slow down so she can relax? We will have a better time and I will feel better if she can help and feels safe with me. Why not let her help?" I am creating an alternative internal dialogue, exploring possibilities and finding a way to feel better, not through changing her, but by adjusting myself.

5: The Reaction—What I Do

Old: I firmly say "I know!", sigh heavily or go cold and silent. I shift from being at ease and "with" her to a defensive stance "against" her.

New: I could openly communicate my feelings:

"You know I get mad when you give me directions." When she reacts to traffic: "I see that and it's okay," or, "Is there a way I could be driving that would help you feel more relaxed?" Even if already upset and not feeling genuine, I am trying new options and willing to experiment with new possibilities.

6: The Consequences—Immediate and Longer-term Fallout

Old: The good mood and fun of the day is gone. Resentments build over the years.

New: We remain engaged in conversation, talk about it and eventually make agreements to enjoy driving together. Perhaps we come to understand our insecurities and issues which show up in other areas of our relationship and throughout our lives.

7: Memories that Arise When I Think About All This

The hurt: I often remember getting lost and feeling scared and helpless on a pre-school class trip to the zoo. Looking at my pattern brought back the memory of when I was lost and afraid in my twenties on a solo trek deep in the Canadian wilderness at dusk. I recalled an early date with my (now) wife, a casual neighborhood walk, when I was unsure of the way back to the house; I can still feel a tight queasiness now when I think of the embarrassment. These events created and confirmed a belief in my inadequacy with directions, as a leader, as a man—a gnawing insecurity behind every endeavor.

The healing: We see in my memories that my mind created a story about myself, taking events as evidence of wholesale inadequacy. I coped by trying to cover up and not let anyone see this horrible defect. Instead, I could openly admit without shame that directions are not my strength. I could ask for and gratefully accept help in this and any area of my life. No one else is expecting perfection. I can embrace other strengths and skills that come easily. I can edit and rewrite my interpretations of and adaptations to my history.

8: The Interpretation—How I Perceive the Situation

Old: Her directions are criticisms. Advice is an attack. She thinks I can't handle this, am no good at this. She doesn't trust me. She is against me. (All of this true for all others.)

New: Here is a more empowering way to see myself that is equally or more true than that negative self-image: I am enthusiastic and fascinated with things. At the zoo, I was entranced with the monkeys longer than were the other kids; I didn't notice they had moved on. In the woods, how impressive that I spent weeks in the mountains in love with the spiritual solitude in nature. I was enraptured with my fiancée; how sweet I was swept away from calculating location. Perhaps my wife knows this about me, accepts and kindly helps me with it. That's a positive spin that has me feeling good about myself and loved when she helps me navigate the car—and life.

9: The Needs—The Basis of All My Actions

To be loved, accepted, supported, praised, needed; to feel that I am competent, capable, trusted.

Behind every upset is a need unmet. Just as a parent must figure out what his crying infant needs to be calm and happy, you must discern and take care of the things that make the difference between agitation and relaxation. Self-soothing is a skill acquired in successful childhood development and must be enhanced as we grow through the increasing demands of life. When my needs are met, I can relax. We may feel weak and vulnerable because we need things, but it works better to fulfill rather than deny needs. More on needs and their connection to patterns in the next chapter and again in the chapter on Desire.

I came to see how my defensive resisting and withdrawing worked directly against fulfilling my needs for love and support, essentially starving myself. This is how patterns spiral and build intensity over time. Not being loved may be less vital than an immediate life-threatening trauma, but it triggers the same survival mechanisms, explaining domestic violence; unfulfilled needs for love turn to hate. Our needs and the beliefs affecting their fulfillment, are keys to unlocking patterns and therefore to our happiness.

10: The Belief—A False Truth

Old: I am incapable, can't handle this or things in general. I am not a man. I'll be found out. She will disrespect me, laugh at me, hate me, leave me.

Beliefs are formed subconsciously, under stress and trauma, as a defensive strategy. They attempt to make sense of and adapt to something difficult or horrible. Reactive patterns are complex coping mechanisms for dealing with a world that is defined by these beliefs. It is the belief that is awakened and taking control when you are triggered, followed by a cascade of automatic reactions which follow. Every reaction and its negative consequences confirm and solidify the belief. The belief, having an urgent survival purpose, is not easily replaced, not until the psyche sees evidence for and trusts a new pathway to safety. We begin by imagining alternative beliefs that lead to fulfilling the needs they serve.

> New Possible Beliefs: I got this. I handle many things well, but don't have to always be right. My sense of direction is not the best and my memory not always perfect. That doesn't make me weak, unlovable, or less of a man. She loves me even with these qualities. I don't have to hide these imperfections (she sees them anyway). I am capable but not perfect. I am lovable as I am. Receiving help is a gift, not a weakness.

The Whole Picture

Why did I suffer so long from the belief that my wife was criticizing me, seeing me as incompetent and trying to control me? This pattern might have repeated for the rest of my life, continually reinforcing negative feelings and creating distance between us. She was simply trying to take care of herself and me! But her behavior triggered—awakened and revealed—my insecurities. Under that brain fog of subconscious defense, I believed it to be an attack when all the same events could have had me feeling loved and supported when viewed through the belief in my competence and seeing her as a careful and helpful partner. My perception was filtered through the subconsciously retained memories of my parents' relationship, my social fears and failures, all of my lifelong attempts to be accepted and loved by women and to understand what "being a man" meant to me. Those historically shaped thoughts created a belief in a particular "reality" and then a defensive reaction to that mentally constructed world.

My Bigger Problem—The World through this Same Lens

I'd like to think my reactive pattern occurs with only one person in this one setting. I'd be wrong. The belief in my inadequacy is the window through which I see everything. I came to see that *any* challenge to my being right, anyone telling me what to do and nearly any offer of support triggered my defensive responses which are many. My wife enjoys calling me a "rulebreaker." I nonetheless have a good life, but it has been much harder than necessary. My self-therapy work continues to be consciously cultivating opposites of the ten factors above, using each step as an exit ramp from the pattern. Accepting my imperfection, seeing authority as support, accepting help.

Re-programming

Computers can be re-programmed and so can our minds. I've shared with you my analysis of this one pattern, based on clues I gathered over time. My hope is that you can solve and resolve yours much faster. There are more significant problems and more terrifying traumas than those I shared here, but self-healing begins wherever you are. My history did not change but my reality did; yours can too.

Your Turn—Identify a Pattern

As you will see in later chapters, which explore the therapeutic use of emotion, distressing feelings indicate a problem and seek a solution. Identify the times you get upset, emotional, angry, or afraid. Their re-occurrence helps you become aware of them. (If you don't think you have any, ask someone who knows you well.) Put your reactive pattern into a cause-and-effect or when-then statement, like these examples from my clients.

> When my mother (or anyone) criticizes me—I become furious and can't speak for days.

> When my partner raises his voice—I get scared and quit talking to him for two or three days.

> When I think of the way my father treated me—I feel sad and can't get out of bed.

> When I think about my career—I feel depressed and don't do well at work.

> When I look at my body in the mirror—I feel disgusted and go eat something.

> When my boyfriend broke up with me—I felt sad and depressed for a year. I still don't feel like dating or trying again.

> When I fight with my wife—I feel hopeless that

things will ever get better and start drinking. Other times I get mad and yell insults at her.

When I want to have sex and my partner refuses—I feel rejected and lonely and go sit in the basement, smoke pot and play video games.

Notice in each description there is first something one sees, hears, or thinks—the trigger. Then there is a feeling, an emotional response to that stimulus. Next is a reaction, some behavior. Write one or more of your "when-then" statements in this form: When X happens, I feel Y and then I do Z.

When _____,
I feel _____,
and then I _____.

X is the trigger; Y is the emotion that is activated; Z is the reaction. There may be several of each in your pattern. Make it a simple sentence, as in the examples.

///

Now Show Me Yours—Break Down the Steps of the Pattern

There is much more to this sequence, micro-steps that happen so fast and automatically that they have become invisible, but the more awareness you have of the sequence, the better able you will be to change the outcome. Are you ready to face and break yours? (My editor said no one likes to do homework, but I said they gotta do the work!) You came to this work wanting change, so fill in more of the cascade of reactions in your pattern. Create your own worksheet from the numbered list below or download Reactions Worksheet at: www.emotional-liberation.com/resources.

The Scenario: Your X + Y + Z statement and a longer narrative.

The Pattern Name: _____

1—Calm Before the Storm (positive feelings and thoughts)

2—The Trigger (what initiates the sequence— any and all cues that set you off)

3—The Feelings (emotion)

4—The Thoughts (what runs through your head)

5—The Reactions (what you do)

6—The Consequences (the immediate and longer-term fallout)

7—Memories/Related History (other and earliest events that may come to mind)

8—The Interpretation (your spin on the situation)

9—The Needs (the essential things required for your well-being that were not met then and you are trying to get now)

10—The Belief (the subconscious program concluded from an earlier event and which prevents fulfillment of the needs)

Describe as many of the individual steps as you can name. They may occur in any order and so rapidly and automatically that any specific piece may take time to become aware of. You are bringing an unconscious habit pattern into conscious awareness. Fill in as many details in each area as you can, leaving space to add realizations that will come later. It is helpful to close your eyes and replay the scenes in your mind as clearly as you can. Like a puzzle or solving a crime, each piece or bit of information is a clue that leads to the final solution. In this chapter, we are using a cognitive approach, adding later the mindful power of intuition and emotion to find more that you don't yet know that you know.

Having identified individual details from the cascade of thoughts, feelings and behaviors that occur when triggered, each step will be a pivot point, an opportunity to regain conscious control. Mentally walk through each step and create optional responses to each habitual reaction. Imagining preferred sequences creates new neural pathways that lay the foundation for new behaviors. These options will come to mind after the pattern occurs, then as it happens, until you eventually re-direct to the "new" in real time.

//

Patterns in Partnership—When We Trigger Each Other

In all relationships, our individual patterns will create a combined pattern that becomes interlocked and intensifies over time. This combination can be particularly tricky to detect and disarm, in part because we see theirs but not ours and each pattern is reinforced by the other; we dig in to defend and to win. Blaming the other or thinking you are responsible for their reactions will also keep you both stuck. When the patterns are identified, the intense emotions and bruised egos make it difficult to disengage. Taking personal responsibility— not blame—for your reactions, their underlying wounds and your needs are crucial to moving forward. You can resolve your side of the equation even if they don't budge and often, you may heal the whole situation through your clarity. Identifying your part is where you can affect change, so let's look at an example of interlocked patterns that I hope will help you identify any in which you are engaged.

Diego has a subconscious belief that he is stupid and ineffective. When anything goes wrong or when someone doesn't like something in their own life, he believes it to be his fault. The more he cares for the person, the more responsibility he takes for their happiness. If he is criticized, blamed, or made wrong, the guilt and shame become torturous. This pattern was created by his mother, who blamed him for her unhappiness. His partner, Kit, is the youngest of 4, whose siblings overpowered and bullied her. She often felt unheard, unimportant and was unable to get what she needed. Her subconscious belief is that she will never get her needs met. She came into her marriage as we all do, expecting to get a lot of what she needed from her partner, not knowing that her subconscious belief was that she wouldn't. Diego was ready to take the blame.

Many years into the relationship, Kit was dissatisfied with him and he blamed himself for their troubles, further blocking his ability to be a good partner. His withdrawal felt to her like old memories of being bullied.

Both of them had done therapy and otherwise worked on self-awareness and shared a sincere desire to learn and grow— excellent conditions for change. A little outside coaching enabled them to see and talk about these patterns. Next, taking responsibility and control of their pattern, rather than taking all the blame or displacing it onto their partner, were all crucial steps. Then came the hard, inner work to understand and change their thoughts and feelings. Diego's job was to consciously build his sense of self-esteem and not blame himself for Kit's part of the troubles. Kit's work was to take responsibility for her needs and break the cycle of her discontent, to learn that she could now be fulfilled rather than remain in the cycle of frustration that occurred when she was young. As they both took control of their beliefs and could realize when they were triggered, they moved away from those reactions. They became happier as individuals and could more clearly see if the relationship could work.

Here are a few examples of mutually triggering patterns.

> *"When my dog whines to get fed, I get irritated and vent my frustration and feel better when I punish by not feeding him. He whines louder and barks, I get madder until..."*

> *"When we agree to leave at 2:00 and my wife is late, I get angry, raise my voice and criticize. She gets afraid, goes silent and slows down, making us later and me more upset."*

> *"I am an adult, but when my mother asks if I have done this, thought about that and asks many questions trying to micromanage my life, I get angry and tell her to shut up. She just wants to connect with me, so this hurts her, whereupon she pushes harder. It all makes me feel incapable and I find myself not taking care of things very well. Hence, she interferes again."*

Describe combined patterns you have with at least three different people. Use the X + Y = Z statement for what occurs from your point of view and again from theirs.

Working with an Interlocked Pattern

Knowing that we all have these everyday insanities, go with compassion for all, persistence to change, determination to live in peace and patience to get there. When a partner (intimate, business-related, friend, or relative) is a significant source of your triggers, it is a natural reflex to blame them.

You can become trigger free unilaterally, with no cooperation from or change in your partner! With a strong nervous system, healthy boundaries, excellent emotional skills and communication, it is possible to be safe and calm when others are not. But don't give up on cooperation and mutual healing. Like trauma, every challenging interaction is a chance to learn, to grow and to heal each other. Animals can be trained to behave well; can't we? Here are some steps to make.

Ask your partner, or insist if you must, to help you to become trigger free. They have much to gain: they could live and work with a less emotionally reactive person. Explain what you have learned about your pattern. Take ownership rather than place blame for your reactions. The Non-Violent Communication model of Marshall Rosenberg is highly effective and worth studying. "When you [observable, factual action], I feel [your emotions here]. What I want is [positive feelings and interactions—your vision of a great relationship]. So, would you please [a request that, if accepted, would not trigger you and indeed meet a need]." This structure is brilliantly designed not to put others on the defensive—your feelings and reactions are not their fault—and garner their cooperation because they likely share your higher vision for a better relationship. This model requires you to do the work of recognizing what you want and asking for it.

Is your partner willing to look at their pattern? You can fill in the sequence steps with them. You already know what you do to trigger them. Once the pattern is identified, one or both will realize the next time it happens. When calmer heads return you can discuss and will learn more. Humor helps! Make it a game between you to kindly catch yourself and the other in the act of reacting. Create alternative exit strategies together. When long-standing patterns build hurt and resentment, it can be hard to want to cooperate or make any effort. You may need to take some form of a break in your interactions to de-escalate, make space to get clear and restore your energy, confidence and hope. When you are back in your power and feeling centered, you can even lead the way out of the swamp, knowing that every bit of strength that you share will come back to benefit you in and outside of the relationship.

Defusing a Conflict Cycle—Another Example

Mark has a laidback personality, while his wife Joan is passionate and active. Their frequent conflict cycle happened recently when a matter arose at their daughter's school. In their discussion, Joan was very concerned and was speaking with intensity, while Mark didn't think it was serious at all. As always, she felt he didn't care and that she was not important to him. Her response had him feeling criticized, wrong and generally a failure. He withdraws, further triggering her intensity, which sends him further into retreat.

> Her Belief: I don't matter. Her interpretation of his behavior: You don't hear/see/understand me; you don't care/value/respect me.

> His Belief: I am a failure, therefore unloved/unlovable; you are going to leave me.

> Her Need: To be validated by seeing that others understand and support her concerns.

> His Need: To be accepted by hearing that conflict does not mean abandonment.

By recognizing their own need as well as their partner's, each was willing to avoid the other's trigger, help meet their needs and ask the other how to do the same for them. Mark tried to respond with more attention and enthusiasm, better matching her energy level even if he was not upset about the matter. He told her he didn't want to retreat anymore and asked for her help by saying she's not mad at him, but at the issue, that she loves him, but we disagree right now. If possible, could she discuss issues in a calmer, kinder tone? When feeling triggered, he now says, "I hear you and I am feeling triggered right now. I am not retreating, but I need a few minutes to breathe and calm down before we continue.

Be Bigger—Stay Off Their Trigger

Subconsciously or on purpose, once we know how to upset a partner, we will do just that when we are hurt and unhappy. Misery loves company, so look for times when you provoke your partner. While it feels satisfying and powerful to upset someone by taking revenge for what they (or your parents) did to you, it is ultimately self-sabotage. A gift you can give yourself and your partner is to stay off of their triggers. Like land mines, get to know where they are and stay away from those words and behaviors. Don't think they deserve your generosity? Then make a deal: I'll stay off of your triggers if you stay off of mine. Then, when one or both of us does get activated, we will take a cooling-off period before trying to work things out.

Just as "good fences make good neighbors," clear agreements really must be established if there is to be peace. Behind every conflict are unfulfilled expectations with no agreement. Take any issue, sit down and negotiate to reach an explicit agreement—even if it takes years. You won't get everything you want. You have to give up some preferences in exchange for the privilege of sharing life with another person. And they must accept some things they don't love about you if there is to be peace. Once made, stick to your agreements, share without anger when they are not kept by you or the other. It is a shared learning process that takes time. I have seen the making and keeping of agreements work wonders.

Help Others Meet Their Needs

Want peace in any relationship? Work to know their needs as well as your own. We all have trauma-related essential needs. Knowing them and the particular way your partner can receive them can act like magic to soften and endear them to you. An example and systematic method for this is *The Five Love Languages*, by Gary Chapman. It is well worth your time to learn and practice in your relationships, intimate or otherwise. The general premise is that we all have needs— think of love as a broad category of needs, including kindness, support, respect, connection—and specific individual ways we can receive them. When you know the key actions that unlock your partner's ability to feel loved, they naturally become a more loving person to you in return. Serving the needs of others is self-serving; it will benefit your life tremendously.

Triage—Where to Start for the Most Benefit

Just like the airlines, which instruct you to put on your mask first so you are in shape to help others, take care of your needs first. Then you can handle many things without coming unglued. We, our patterns and our triggers are humbling but not so complicated. We get upset when our needs aren't met. You can't get everything you want when and how you demand, but you can always (learn to) get what you need. The best thing you can do for others is to take care of yourself. Recognize what you need to be your best self and learn how to take care of those needs well enough to not so easily feel desperately upset—to not get triggered and react—in a moment when the world is not cooperating as you wish. Know your patterns and their root cause—the needs that trigger you and the old, trauma-created beliefs that stand in the way. Imagine a world in which you, parents, bosses, politicians and leaders don't complain, blame, or blow up. You can reach that trigger-free future. It might be the single best thing you can do for world peace.

Chapter 2

Trauma:
Source of Pain, Patterns and Transformation

We're All Recovering from Something

It may be the cutting remark your mother made five minutes ago that got your blood boiling or the way she criticized you as a child that left you feeling not good enough to please her. You may feel mildly anxious on a date or deeply disturbed by the memories of a sexual violation many years ago. When our peace is disturbed, when a physical or psychological wound occurs, there is a whole body/mind defensive response that arises to protect and defend. We become agitated emotionally; react, attack, or withdraw to find a way out of the discomfort. It may take minutes to years to regain our pre-event state of calmness, clarity and dignity. Challenging events happen to everyone every day. They change us in ways that can diminish our sense of who we are, how safe we are, alter what we believe about the world and expect from our relationships and can cripple our ability to function effectively to handle life. We are all walking wounded.

You think you have problems today, but your ancestors were naked in the wilds full of storms and beasts with just a stick for defense. Survival has always been hard—traumatic—for all living things. Through 500 million years of animal life and the nearly 1 million years of rapid human brain development, we evolved to handle and recover from trauma. The reptilian, mammalian and advanced human parts of your brain contribute their physical monitoring, emotionally regulating and intellectually creative capacities to your ability to adapt to and cope with whatever hardship comes your way. Our understanding of bacteria and the immune system led to great improvements in physical health. We are now in a period of discovery about our innate psychological healing abilities.

By doing this Emotional Liberation work, you are part of these discoveries. The next steps in the process are to recognize trauma and its effects, accept it with compassion and without shame, examine it through a model of empowerment and apply healing techniques.

"Until recently, when folks would talk about trauma, I thought trauma had to be something huge like a natural disaster, war, rape, or near-death accident. I didn't realize that my experience of physical and verbal abuse, mind games and psychological warfare "qualified" as trauma since I perceived it as making me stronger, shaping me to be who I am as a more compassionate person. However, I seem to come to a familiar theme when meditating on these unresolved issues around my father. Needing his love so badly, being angry for not getting it, feeling undeserving of it, then projecting that onto all my relationships—including with God. I need love so badly but always get rejected and am then so angry about it. This also spills over into my business as an extension of myself. I pour my heart into it and when things don't go as planned, I take it as an attack on me, a rejection and confirmation that I am undeserving—all conditioning from childhood. I came to Emotional Liberation to heal what I now understand as the "trauma" of betrayal by my caregivers, situations I faced but couldn't deal with as a child—nor even now as an adult in similar situations. I understand now that they are still open wounds that need to heal." —Amita

Safety First!

I invite you to understand better how life's hurtful events have affected you so the past no longer robs you of confidence, success and happiness. Reading about, recalling and discussing trauma can itself be re-traumatizing. On the road to befriending uncomfortable feelings, go at your own pace, stay safely in control of how far and how fast you dip into the watery world of your dear emotions. Unlike before, you now have an opportunity to be in control. Get whatever support— from a friend, group, or professional—that helps you feel safe to do this work. Know that millions of people before you have taken this dive into themselves and come out clean and bright. Research has found that trauma lives in the body as well as the mind and that by engaging memory with physical and emotional feelings, the lingering effects of trauma can be released. Be kind, careful and curious on this journey of discovery and growth.

Trauma as a Catalyst for Growth and Change

Wounds can heal. Scar tissue is tougher than untouched skin. Healing an injury requires creative adaptation, learning to use our body differently, developing other muscles, letting go of how we used to be and finding new strength. Who knew one could paint with their toes or run a race in a wheelchair with their arms until a terrible challenge found a way through? At the cellular level, genes break, merge and mutate to evolve continually; negative pressures create incredible variety and possibility. You have felt trapped by your past, but you can recover. In the short term, recovery means you get through your day with ease, the upsets of others don't upset you, you handle challenge and tragedy with resilience and hardiness without being drained, overwhelmed or defeated.

Stress is either a destructive force or a positive pressure and a stimulus to grow. When used positively, challenges become a possibility for recovery from the tragedies of our personal and collective histories.

Trauma occurs to initiate growth and change. We can take a negative thing and put it to positive use. We're not talking about positive thinking but real transformation; to go through pain to emerge stronger, wiser, victorious. You don't have to believe this is possible to start, though the knowledge that your trauma can make you stronger adds hope, willingness and motivating optimism to your efforts. Rather than just a nice idea, this is the outcome achieved by those doing this work; you can do it, too.

The following will be our functional definition of trauma. Listen for how it can also serve as a measure of progress in your journey of recovery:

> When I have grown to know now what I didn't know then, so I can do what I couldn't do then, to handle and make similar situations okay now that weren't okay then, I have learned the lesson and achieved the evolutionary purpose of that trauma. To this degree, I now have positive effects from the experience; I am at peace with it. I am healed.

Our generalized use of the word "trauma" does not diminish or dishonor the suffering of those with severe trauma. Instead, we honor the commonality of trauma at all levels so that it does not go unattended. By recognizing and normalizing trauma, we hope to take away any stigma and fear so we can all learn and grow from it. It will help to define its many types, sources and effects. It will give you context to see where you are in the full spectrum of traumatic experience and make more apparent connections to its effects.

In daily use, the word trauma can refer to both the events and its effects, as in *"I had a severe trauma at age 6. I was traumatized and now I live with trauma."* Here is a broad definition of trauma I use for its recognition of emotion: psychological trauma is a type of damage to the mind that occurs as a result of a distressing event. Trauma is often the result of an overwhelming amount of stress that exceeds one's ability to cope or integrate the emotions involved with that experience. The second part of this book will give you the ability to more than cope with the emotions of distressing events: they will be the agents of your healing. They are integral to our ability to cope with current stressful events and process the past.

Types of Trauma—Recognize Yours

What happened to you? As you read these descriptions of the varieties of traumatic experiences, write a list of any of these words you identify with and all specific events you recall. I suggest brief descriptions that simply identify experiences at this point instead of longer retellings of each story. If it is uncomfortable to do so, you can stop anytime or not do it at all, but it is part of a process you will acclimate to in time.

Acute Trauma: A single overwhelming experience and its effects

> A man in a ski mask broke into my home and raped me.
>
> My family was in a car wreck; my twin sister died next to me.
>
> I survived a mass shooting at my school.
>
> I lived in terror through Hurricane Katrina.

Repetitive Trauma: Exposure to several, possibly "milder," but ongoing adverse experiences or conditions and their cumulative effects

> I trembled in my room many nights while my father yelled angrily at my mom.

> I was a slow learner. The kids and many teachers made fun of me in class.

> My father left us when I was three. After that, my mother was depressed and neglectful.

> I grew up in a dangerous and violent neighborhood.

> As a person of color, I've always felt mistreated.

Complex Trauma: A combination of prolonged, intense experiences, especially within a close relationship or at the hands of caregivers expected to nurture

> My mother was manic-depressive. We never knew when we were going to get a treat or a beating.

> My creepy step-father did a lot of inappropriate things to me over the years.

Developmental Trauma: The intensified impact of all adverse experiences and toxic stress on infants and children when brain, behavior and beliefs are formed

> When I was six, my father died and my mom had to work all the time. I became the "mother," doing everything for my three brothers.

> My father was serious and distant. There was no affection or encouragement in our house.

> As a baby, I remember being hungry, cold and scared at night, but no one ever came when I cried.

Vicarious Trauma: An empathetically absorbed experience of and reactions to someone else's trauma

> My son went through a year of terrible cancer treatments with low expectations of survival. He's okay now, but I will never be the same.

> As a paramedic, I see gruesome things every day. Those visions haunt me at night.

> Following the news gave me constant anxiety, so I stopped watching any of it.

> My mother sat in a drunken stupor every afternoon in her chair. Made me depressed.

Intergenerational and Cultural/Historical Trauma: Effects of trauma absorbed through socialization—the cumulative messages that surround us from birth and (evidence shows) passed on through our parents' DNA.

> My mother was young during the Depression, but all of us kids still scrimp and save or work like crazy all the time.

> When I visited the National Lynching Memorial in Alabama...I could just feel centuries of hatred and fear in my bones that I have thought myself many times, growing up in the white man's world.

> My great grandmother talked about the Holocaust and today my Jewish community is a major target of hate crimes.

> Men have no idea about the harassment women face.

Has anyone NOT had one or many of these experiences? Research estimates up to 90% of us have experienced one or more forms of trauma in our lives. That is clinically defined trauma; further down the spectrum of intensity, life's many slights, disappointments and challenges affect everyone. Recognizing that these broadly-defined phenomena touch us all, we realize the importance of bringing fully online our ability to recover and grow from these inevitable experiences. We can upgrade the line, "Whatever doesn't kill you makes you stronger" to, "Every adverse event is an irritating grain of sand until we make it into a pearl," or simply, "Every hardship creates an opportunity for growth."

The Effects of Trauma

All that happened to you before this very moment is in the past; it's not happening right now. Your history wouldn't be a problem but for the after-effects that linger long after a traumatic experience. As you read just some of the symptoms below, make a separate list of your symptoms. They may not seem related to anything that happened, just list all past and current behaviors you identify in your life. Don't be overly critical or judgmental; be in compassionate inquiry mode to better know yourself. These symptoms may not all be due to trauma, but look at them compared to a healthy, happy, well-adjusted and fully self-actualized person with the question, why is this happening?

Physical: Do you have difficulties with food, sleep, sex, high and low energy swings, undiagnosable body issues, strong dislikes of your physical features, frequently find yourself in environments that are stressful, chaotic, harmful, unhealthy?

Emotional: Do you have mood swings, cyclic or ongoing depression, extreme sensitivity and vulnerability, panic attacks? Do you frequently feel anxious and overwhelmed, irritated, debilitating shame, or that you are damaged or defective? Do you experience emotional numbness, a need to withdraw to feel safe, frequent and intense reactions, heavy self-criticism, low self-confidence? Are you strongly self-critical, think you are a terrible person, work hard to please others and avoid conflict at high personal cost?

Behavioral: Do you have self-harming habits, constant frustrations or frequent failures, recurring relationship difficulties, obsessive and addictive behaviors, a tendency to isolate?

Mental and Cognitive: Do you fixate on events and memories, have unstoppable churning thoughts, blank spots in your history, difficulty making decisions, anxiety and confusion about what to do, severe lack of focus, massive negative and depressive thoughts, or thoughts of hopelessness?

The Cause-and-Effect Connection

Did you name some of these symptoms of trauma in your patterns from Chapter 2? Perhaps now you see more that have shown up in you or others you know. What keeps happening that robs you of health and happiness? Things you wanted to change but can't seem to, or worse, have come to accept as usual? Do people mistreat and take advantage of you, or always bug you? Does the life you want seem just out of reach, getting what you want beyond your control? Can't speak up, but wish you could? Start but can't finish things or give up easily? Want a relationship, but it never works out? Do things keep getting worse instead of better?

While many of these conditions can arise from any number of sources, consider the idea that you may be suffering not from personal defects, bad luck, or genetics. They are responses to trauma. Your adverse experiences directly shaped you by altering your thinking, expectations, beliefs and reactions to your environment. With few exceptions, you were not born with these; they arose in response to adverse experiences. They are adaptive attempts to cope with stress.

The good news is, you can upgrade your responses to stress. Look at your list of negative effects, then begin to envision being free of them. Having lived with those effects for so long—short-fused temper, withdrawal and isolation, over-responsible control-taking—they may seem to be permanent aspects of your personality. By recognizing and working with the mental, emotional and physical imprints of those experiences, you can process and release their effects as a sewage treatment plant does, releasing clean water in the end. Beneath the impacts of trauma awaits your fully self-actualized life.

How long does recovery take? Generally, recovery time is proportional to the degree of the negative impact that adverse experiences leave on us; the more significant the wound, the longer the healing, just as with physical injury. Healing accelerates with focus, effort, nurturing environments and support and practical tools. Moreover, as we increase understanding and use of our innate self-healing capacities, I believe this will no longer be so. When I was young, people remained in bed for long periods after surgery. Now, due to better understanding of the body's ability to recover, doctors get you up and walking the next day. Just so, we will find psychological recovery capabilities far beyond current norms. Continue to do all of the exercises in this book. Each one can assist your self-purification over time.

Trauma-Amplifying Factors

Each adverse experience throughout your life shocked your sensitive self and rocked your world order. Have compassion for that earlier version of yourself who was shocked, overwhelmed and hurt. Rather than the guilt or self-blame that sometimes tries to explain away trauma, understand with empathy the conditions that increase the impact of painful events. Note that some are mechanical, while others are a matter of interpretation, how you perceive what is happening.

Intensity of the Event

Was the earthquake a 7.2 or a tremor? Was the wreck a 70 m.p.h smash-up or a 25 m.p.h. rear-ender? Did you hear your father yelling at your brother downstairs, or did he hit you directly? Did your father spank to punish, slap, or hit hard with his fist?

Duration and Frequency

Did it disturb your security to see your mother drunk once, or was it every night? Were you bullied by one guy in first grade or every year through high school? Was it chaotic or dangerous in your home for years until you could get out on your own? Did an illness or disability last for years?

Physical Harm Left

Related to intensity, did the bruise heal in a week or leave you with a permanent disability?

Size and Power Disadvantage

Was your abuser a huge adult male and you were 3, 16, 28, or 45? Did your work peer comment on your performance, or was it the CEO from corporate and the email copied everyone or was at the annual retreat? Did the full weight of the law, social bias, or nature come down on you?

Exposure

Did a boy see your underwear on the playground, or did nude photos go viral? Did "I wanted to die" embarrassment happen with one friend or on stage in front of the whole school?

Suddenness and Unexpectedness

Did your 90-year-old relative die slowly, or was your child

gone in a tragic accident? Did you know the thing was coming so you could prepare mentally and physically or was it an out-of-nowhere shock? Did you think your relationship was great only to find they cheated and left you without notice?

Confusion/Incomprehension

Early sexual violation by a caregiver is deeply confusing. They may say it is okay, but it feels horrible. Overwhelming events that violate your reality and are beyond comprehension and confusion and fear that disrupt the previous worldview, leave us in unstable limbo. The mind grasps false explanations like, "It's my fault" or, "It never happened."

Intentional vs. Accidental

Surviving a hurricane is traumatic. If you believe God was punishing you, the effect is worse than if you see it as a random act of nature. Someone attacking you vengefully is worse than an accident, even if the resulting harm is the same.

Freedom of Movement and Choice

Could you get away, or were you physically constrained? Were you too young to speak, or call for help, or to know there were laws and hotlines? Were you in a country, culture, or role that socially limited your freedom?

//

A Self-Assessment of Life Events' Impact

As an act of compassionate understanding for yourself, examine the factors that gave events in your life their impact. When we have thoughts like, *it wasn't so bad, other people had it much worse* and *I shouldn't complain*, they may stand in the way of recognizing harm and its effects. It has become clear that acknowledging harm is an essential step toward healing it. This is a moment to dive in, feel, get angry and fight back with real recognition of how things affected you. In the grid, put three troubling events in your life—numbered events 1, 2 and 3—of varying types, like parents' divorce, how you were treated in school, a damaging accident or lengthy addiction. Below them, rate the strength of each factor, 0 being no effect at all and 10 being the maximum imaginable. Then add each column for a total score.

Factor	1-	2-	3-
Intensity			
Duration and Frequency			
Physical Harm			
Size and Power Disadvantage			
Exposure			
Suddenness/Unexpectedness			
Confusion/Incomprehension			
Intentional vs. Accidental			
Freedom of Movement/Choice			
Total Magnitude of Impact			

You may feel activated—charged up—after doing that review. Discharge the emotional energy with some deep breathing, strong exercise, a calming walk, meditation. You may want to shout!

Can you better understand why things hurt so much? This shows how a seemingly mild event you might downplay or dismiss can deeply hurt you. An experience that looks objectively minor can have an outsized impact depending on the conditions surrounding it. Do the scores seem proportional to how past events affect you to this day? That helps us understand how trauma touches everyone. Fortunately, other factors help diminish the after-effect of adverse experiences.

///

Resilience—Trauma-Mitigating Conditions You Can Grow

Resilience refers to the capacity to handle stress, recover and even thrive despite trauma. It is about how well we can manage changing conditions, adapt, maintain equilibrium and master our circumstances. Typically, more severe trauma results in more significant disability, but some individual qualities and attitudes make people more or less affected by the same event. While these traits vary widely among individuals, they are not fixed and limited; resilience can be learned and increased by intention. Here are some of these stress-handling, trauma-mitigating factors. You may feel unlucky that you weren't born with some of these, but you can develop them in many creative ways. Here we add just a few examples to get your resilience-building underway.

Relationships are a primary factor. Whatever the past and present quality of relationships, make positive connections with others. Be with those who value you. Ask for and accept support. Be in a group, volunteer, be a good friend and share yourself openly when it is safe to do so. Build a positive self-image (see Chapter 11, on Shame). Take good care of yourself with kindness and your health with good habits. Make plans and take action toward improvements. Keep learning about yourself and what you need to be happy (see Chapter 5, on Desire). Accept that life brings difficulties, but keep doing what you can. Learn to manage your intense feelings and impulses—that is what this book is all about!

Advice to have hope, confidence, self-esteem and other positive attitudes when you are down and not feeling it can sound unfair or impossible. To know that anyone can actively increase these qualities is at least a place to start. Some factors, like emotional sensitivity and nervous system strength, may be inborn. But there are ways to improve whatever you have, such as yoga and diet for the nerves, meditation for focus and mental control, personal growth work for behavioral changes and spiritual work for attitudes and beliefs. Sometimes our pain has to become greater than our inertia and fears to motivate change. And if things are going well already, that's an excellent time to develop resilience against future challenges.

Positives Neutralize Negatives

Each of us responds uniquely to situations because the impact is mainly about perception and perception involves genes, socialization and other personal histories. How you perceive an experience and the beliefs through which you filter it affects the lasting impact it will have on you. This same variable, mental agency, gives you the ability to take back control of the stories you tell yourself about what happened, what it means, what you expect and how you respond. Our survival-oriented brain retains impressions of adverse events more strongly than the positive ones to avoid similar pain in the future. That's why one repeats positive affirmations and prayers, why we tell tales of noble virtues again and again, why aspirants seek high spiritual values with determination for years. So these positives have a chance of sticking! Positive neural pathways can replace previously imprinted negative thought-feeling habits, but it takes work.

If you take the overall effect of positive experiences in your life, minus the cumulative impact of negative experiences—weighted more heavily by childhood and severity—you get a reliable predictor of your psychological health and overall well-being. Lack of control to help oneself dramatically increases the negative impact of any situation. Conversely, nurturing, understanding, loving care and support decrease the detrimental effects of an event. Happily, whatever conditions made it worse back then, those same conditions can heal any harm when received now. If safety or love were scarce then, you can find them now. And fortunately, you can give them to yourself.

To effectively heal painful memory and affect, the positive replacements must be more than thoughts. You must have a "felt" experience, emotionally and somatically. Uplifting and nurturing truths spoken, repeated, chanted and sung with the power of voice and feelings have a much more significant effect. Mass in grand cathedrals was one technology developed to bring higher inspiration and aspiration to the laboring masses by vividly touching all the body's senses, the mind with lofty thoughts and the spirit with mysteries. There are simpler and more private ways to achieve the same effects. Multi-dimensional experience embeds in your nervous and glandular systems—it is real, just as negatively shocking experiences register at all levels of your being. Do you have such practices in your life? There are lots of choices out there, systems, groups and gurus; experiment and find things that work for you. Try this simple sample of your power to release past pain by focusing on—and feeling—good stuff.

Accentuate the Positive to Balance Your Reality

Draw a line down the center of a piece of paper. On the right side, write a name for one or two bad experiences in your life that remain unpleasant to remember. On the left side, list at least a dozen pleasant events that are enjoyable to remember.

Pleasant Memories	Unpleasant Memories
A loving grandparent	Alcoholic or raging parent
My first pet	Death of a pet

My home or room	Being the new/weird kid
Summer vacations	Parents fighting/divorce
Best friend/First love	Any betrayal/heartbreak

If life has been hard it will take some time and digging to remember them, but they happened, or you wouldn't still be here. From recent to childhood memories, sweet, pleasurable, moments, acts of kindness you received or gave, smiles or kind words you remember, the pure warmth of the sun, beauty of nature, time with a pet, small or grand, write no fewer than twelve and add to the list any time. When finished, look over the list. Isn't the one on the right more vivid or remembered more easily and often, especially the more traumatic it was? While you may not remember those on the left as frequently or as vividly, your mind tends to believe events on the right define your life and dismiss those on the left. Are you, in fact, right now resisting, rejecting, or skeptical that this whole exercise is silly and won't work? Those are self-fulfilling thoughts protecting the status quo. We're working to change that.

Now choose your favorite pleasant memory. Close your eyes, breathe deeply, relax and remember that enjoyable experience as vividly as you can. Include all of your senses. What did you see, hear, touch, smell and taste? Re-live each sensation. How did it all make you feel? Feel that again now. Amplify any enjoyable emotions like you are turning up a light dimmer-switch. Let your body start to gently move with the memory in a pleasant way, holding yourself, gently rocking, or fully re-enacting the scene. Don't be shy; let yourself enjoy your movement and sensations. Or equally important to know, observe your unwillingness or seeming inability to enjoy. Start humming, singing, talking to yourself and others in the memory. Talk of love and gratitude, whatever you want to say and hear from them.

Try it again with another memory and revisit these experiences often. The remembered event is itself a new, positive experience and each one tips the scale in your mind to a more positive story about your life. The more wholly engaged in a full-body/mind/emotional experience, the more successfully your nervous system generates new neural pathways and behavioral patterns. Research shows that the proportion of favorable to negative experiences largely determines how we live today. Go out and make as many fresh, real-time positive experiences as you can. Love heals! Rewrite the story you tell yourself.

Studies of resilience show that when loving-kindness is also present, the effects of traumatic experiences are diminished. Most often it is not, but getting kindness, love and support—or any of your needs—even decades after an adverse experience, heals trauma and its effects. Since you can be kind and compassionate with yourself, realize the power you have now to repair what happened back then. Give yourself what you need; it's simple, immediate and always available. While you can't forever control outside harm, you can manage your recovery. Taking care of your needs also resolves everyday upsets. Let's look at the connection.

Connecting Triggers—An Upset Is a Need Not Met

Come back to the work and the worksheet you did with triggers and patterns in Chapter 1. Why do those particular triggers set you off? You were born with the fear of falling and drowning, but not with fear of intimacy or speaking up. You learned those along the way from something that went badly. In going through that analysis of a pattern, you likely had some earlier memories. Common to both your current patterns and past traumas are unfulfilled needs. The things that upset you are an entry point into understanding yourself and healing the wounds that are at the source of your reactions.

Begin with any of your emotional reactions. Underlying every one will be a need that is not getting met. The satisfying of that need might quickly solve your upset if it were not for its connection to one, or probably many, similar previous events in your history. Let's take a fresh look at trauma as any event large or small in which our needs—physical or psychological—went unfulfilled, most often in a very threatening and seemingly impossible way. In those earlier events, you created beliefs about the availability of your needs and the likelihood of getting them. These adaptive mental constructs create a lasting sense of scarcity and, paradoxically, block your current ability to take care of yourself in a way that brings peace and happiness. By unraveling the knot of beliefs that prevent needs-fulfillment, we can be free of reactions *and* process unresolved trauma.

Babies cry when they are uncomfortable: there is something they need that will bring them back to contentment. It is the same for all of us. At the base of your present-day patterns is something you need. But your emotional reactions create behavior that is ineffective at fulfilling it. Later, we will show you how to align emotions with intentions, so their energies help you get what you want.

Amelia's Heart Speaks

Amelia lived in constant anger and sadness. Her mother and older sister regularly excluded and mistreated her. As a child, the youngest of three, her mother worked long hours, was seldom home and gave her little if any attention or affection. Her older sister was abusively mean. Her needs for love and safety then were unmet and are still not coming from either of them today. Amelia came to believe she was unworthy of love, which then continued to create that reality after leaving home. Living with a wonderful husband and two beautiful babies in a lovely house, she felt unsafe and unloved. As a powerful business person, her mother and sister still regularly put her down, leaving her in constant anxiety. Her independence and accomplishments did not replace the old belief that she was unworthy and would never be safe or loved.

I asked her to close her eyes and bring to mind the current and childhood hurts of her mother and sister, to feel the emotions and sensations in her body. (Thinking is not enough; she must engage mind, body and emotions.) I guided her to ask her heart to recognize the needs—she said "love." And the belief? She said, "I am not worthy of it." Her habit of continually telling herself what a bad mother, wife, person she is came pouring through her mind, bringing worse feelings. I then asked her to focus on the many sources of love in her life today. With some help, she felt the love of husband, children, friends with whom she can share her feelings, nature, simple pleasures. These flooded her with good feelings.

When her familiar self-loathing thoughts came, I asked her how she can get back to love. She said she could go into her heart and immediately feel better. After a few minutes, I asked her to think of her mother and sister, how they treat her every day. There was no reaction; she remained peaceful and immune to their harm. By letting love in, past her old belief, she filled the need, broke the pattern and resolved the trauma. Of course, to heal fully, she will need to practice and remember all this regularly to create new neural pathways in her brain and enjoy their resulting "new normal" responses.

Again, consider any trauma an event in which needs were not met in a way that felt profoundly threatening to your well-being. It left you harmed, not only through not having what you needed at the time but also left you with a belief about the availability of that need. That belief helped you to make sense of why you didn't get it, but becomes a flawed operating system that directly thwarts future attempts to fill the need. Try using this concept in your own experience now.

//

Feed the Need to Be at Peace

Research shows that trauma lives in and must be released from the body, engaging the muscles, nervous and glandular systems. This next exercise can be intense, inviting you to shake as animals have been observed to do after trauma. Do it on a soft surface and only to the extent that feels safe. You may want to build your energetic output slowly over several sessions.

Sit quietly in a private place. Breathe deeply and slowly, directing yourself to become calmer, fully present and grounded for three full minutes.

Begin to shake your body all over, moving every muscle. Build the intensity as far as you are willing and able. Flop around on the (padded) floor, twisting and turning, shaking limbs and extremities. Use your voice to make any sound that wants to come out: sighs, groans, animal noises, howls. Let emotion flow if it arises: anger, fear, sadness with tears. A piece of energetic drumming music may encourage your movement. Go for at least five minutes or until you are exhausted.

Sit or lie flat and become still. Feel the strength of breath and heartbeat as your body recovers equilibrium. Feel the life-energy moving through your body; relax to allow it to flow. Allow the mind to rest along with the body. Guide yourself back into mental calmness and clarity.

Bring to mind the recurring situation you worked with in the Triggers exercise. Or remember any other recent or recurring situation that upsets you.

Replay this "video" as vividly as possible, seeing, hearing, feeling your body and emotions as they were then while realizing you are actually calm and safe in your body now.

In that situation, ask your body what you needed. Feel for the answer in the body rather than from the mind. Imagine being able to be, have, or do anything that would make you satisfied. Go deeper into your heart to ask it what you want so badly. Imagine the scene now going that way; others do and you get exactly what makes you happy. If you imagine well, you will feel immediate relief. Let that feeling relax your entire being.

Take a deep breath and let it out with a big sigh. Do that again, twice.

Now, remember a situation much earlier in your life that was similar to the one you just went through. Again, involve your senses and feel the emotions, which may be the same. Observe that younger version of yourself from the position of your adult self. Use all the wisdom and kindness of a loving parent.

Can you feel now what that innocent child needed? Was it a physical or emotional need, or both? What did they/you believe about what was happening? About yourself and the world?

Drop down out of your head and into your heart to listen there when you ask, "What is the real truth about me, this need and getting it?"

Ask your body, heart and spirit how to get that same need. Imagine many real ways to get many forms of it.

Is there a similarity between what you needed and didn't get when traumatized and the need(s) you have in present-day upsets?

Continue observing, asking any questions and feeling answers as long as you wish. Then breathe deeply, stretch and come back to the present with your eyes open.

If you identified any needs or beliefs from past or present, add them to your Reactions Worksheet from Chapter 2. Make it your mission to go about getting those needs fulfilled. Proportionately, those familiar triggers will not upset you. Just as a well-fed animal can't be lured into a dangerous situation to obtain food, you won't bite the bait in situations that caught you when you felt empty and unable to handle yourself.

//

Your reactive patterns are the result of overwhelming events which can be used as catalysts for growth and healing. The pattern contains and reveals the whole story: the emotions, the harm, the unmet needs, the adopted beliefs and the specific abilities that were lacking at the time. Those same abilities, utilized today, will save you. Every recurrence gives you a chance to review the trauma, learn and adopt new beliefs and behaviors that will take care of yourself now in ways you couldn't before. Patterns are your own personal *Groundhog Day*. In this 1993 movie, Bill Murray re-lives a day over and over again until he figures out what is causing his unhappiness. In a fun way, it shows how life utilizes painful negative consequences to help us learn how to have the positive experiences we prefer. You don't have to re-live past trauma or in the shadow it casts to create present-day suffering. Mindfully seeing and re-experiencing traumas and reactions leads to compassionate understanding and resolution. And the truth shall set you free!

Chapter 3

Recovery and the Therapy of Self-Awareness

"If every child in the world would be taught meditation, we would eliminate violence from the world in one generation."
—*The Dalai Lama*

Evolving Therapeutic Models

We know a lot about the harm that trauma causes. What have we learned about how to help? As a meditation teacher for 40 years, I found great results when I brought those self-awareness techniques into my mental-health work as a yoga therapist. Science is discovering the same. In the short century or so that we can say mental health became a science, psychologists have been changing their minds about how to, well, change our minds. Freud's psychoanalysis looked at the hidden meaning of our thoughts and what they reveal about us. Beck's Cognitive Behavioral Therapy is a "second wave" of talk therapy that helps to not take our thoughts so seriously and to challenge "automatic negative thoughts." A belief common to all professional approaches in western psychotherapy has been that talking about troubling events, thoughts and feelings can resolve them.

Current brain research is making clear why when I talk about my problems, my "thinking brain" doesn't heal the "emotional brain" that feels angry and afraid. Science is taking us beyond traditional talk therapy and toward a third wave that begins to look like and validate ancient yogic practices of meditation and Buddhist concepts like acceptance and self-compassion. This approach suggests that we develop a relationship with our mind to work together; cooperation with a mind that can otherwise go out of control.

Another wave of treatments growing over the last 70 years is the use of drugs to control our mental/emotional activity. As life-saving as this can be, it may cover up rather than resolve problems: I don't feel so bad; I don't feel much at all. Medical and recreational drugs may support avoidance of the very feelings we need to recognize and solve our problems. Self-awareness—knowing what I feel and why—offers a promise of self-recovery. Mindfulness and other meditation practices increase self-awareness. So, working mindfully with emotions that arise in therapy takes us to the cutting edge of effectiveness. This is what those yogis in caves did and we can too. Enlightenment didn't come right away for them, either. Rather, by paying close attention, realization and liberation grow over time.

The life coaching profession that has blossomed in the last 30 years has brought a more directive, results-oriented approach to counseling. The coaching model includes helping the client find their own answers, having them take action steps to reach their goals and holding them accountable to do so. Again, talking about problems is not enough: personal empowerment, using new skills and changing one's circumstances are all part of healing the past and improving the present. In all these models we see that when we increase awareness—to see and understand what is and what could be—our quality of life can begin to change for the better.

Change Happens through Dawning Self-Awareness

Self-Awareness, as a road to understanding and resolving personal problems, is a process of gradual awakening. As a yoga therapist, my job is to assist a client's process of self-realization. That occurs in clearly identifiable stages. Here is a behavior modification outline I call the Ten Stages of Change, from total unawareness to resolution. I have given each level a name and a client's real-life example. Have in mind the pattern you identified in Chapter 1, or any other issue you have been trying to resolve and see if you recognize any familiar stages. Knowing where you are and next steps will speed you along your way.

1–What Problem? Dysfunction and suffering become normal over time. Not knowing there's a problem keeps it in place. *"Growing up with domestic violence, I never knew anything else, so when my marriage was the same, I lived with that abuse for years, not knowing anything was wrong or that I could do something about it."* Outside information and lifelines are needed.

2–Sick of It. Repetition and pain reach a limit and ability to see there's a problem. *"My mother's criticism and put-downs have continued throughout my life. She can make me feel so bad each time we talk, but my anger has been building—alternating with depression. I am sick of it!"* How long did it go on before you saw what was happening? If you did the Pattern Deactivation Worksheet you now see one clearly. You have others yet to be discovered.

3–Alternatives Appear. Help arrives with new ideas and solutions that bring hope of a better way. *"Attending an ALANON meeting* *blew my mind. Hearing other people who grew up with alcoholic parents tell how they got over their trauma gave me a vision of positive possibilities for my life."* A book (including this one), web searches, a friend's experience and advice, social rights movements that change what is acceptable.

4—See the Promised Land. Knowing something better is possible makes the old ways intolerable, which motivates courage and action. *"For years I'd find the courage to free myself from one toxic relationship only to end up in another, trapped and afraid to speak up and take care of myself. I could see what I needed to do but couldn't stick with it."* This comparative study stage can be quick or last a long time while you learn, gather tools, grow stronger and form ideas for how to change. Repeatedly visualize what you would like to say and do.

"In a book I read on co-dependence, it described exactly what is happening in my marriage. I signed up for a counseling program to figure this out and get over it." Google your situation; somebody has already figured it out and offers skilled help. Decide you want to change, get support that holds you accountable and get to work.

5—It Happened Again! At this stage, new ways are known but not yet used. We are unaware in the moment that we are caught in the automatic behaviors, but realize it sometime later. *"Yesterday, I blew up again. I just don't see it coming and don't realize I am being triggered until much later when I calm down. I know my pattern now, just can't stop it."* Once you realize what happened, meditatively replay the "video" of the incident in your head, then replay it the way you want to think, feel and act next time. New neural pathways will grow until the pattern you imagine can happen one day.

6–Real-Time Realization. With repetition, you become aware that it is happening while it is happening. It's like watching a movie you can't edit, but at least you are self-aware in the moment. *"It was kinda weird just watching myself shut down, knowing what I wanted to say, but once again I couldn't speak. I felt helpless and just let it happen."* You won't yet be able to stop the pattern, but you are learning and close to the change you want.

7–Set the Stage. At calmer times, when not engaged in the behavior, build the circumstance and support that will facilitate life as you envision it. *"I told him not to talk like that to me again. Next time he starts going off, I'm not going to argue and get mad. I'll just hang up or leave until he cools down so we can talk about it."* Communicate, set boundaries with consequences, declare your intentions, get agreements from others and witnesses and other forms of back-up.

8—Successful Shifts. One fine day you are able to exit the pattern and thereby have a better outcome. *"The last two times I felt that rush of sadness, I went to see my friend instead of getting drunk. First time since she died that I could divert that urge and find real support."* At this point there is often a mix of events going unaware, seeing helplessly and sometimes asserting your better self. It takes persistence and courage.

9—The New Normal. The change is complete, at some point effortless. *"When my father starts his thing about how I didn't turn out the way he could be proud of, now I just laugh and jokingly say I feel the same way about him. I now see that his digs are about his pain, not me. I accept and love him for who he is."* It's hard to believe change can take so much time and work, but it's worth it—for the rest of your life and for all those affected.

Where are you along this continuum with a current issue or pattern? Awareness of where you are and where you want to go will shorten the learning curve as you reach for the next levels of your dawning self-awareness.

Know Your Brains—Who's in Charge?

Why is change so much work? And why did the Dalai Lama say meditation is a remedy for the violence that causes our trauma? Knowing a bit about the hardware in your head will help answer these questions and frame the importance of the work with emotions in trauma recovery. The brainstem—your reptilian brain—monitors and controls survival: breath, hunger, sleep. The limbic system—your mammalian brain—deals with the complexities of interacting with the world and others. How it responds changes with experience and is more heavily affected in your early years. Together, this so-called emotional brain's job is to make sure you are okay. It uses and stores sensory and emotional memories to protectively react quickly to similar sights, sounds and people; trauma excites it. What it recalls feels real right now—which we can use for recovery—but is why you shut down or blow up when a partner reminds you of a mean parent.

The prefrontal cortex (PFC)—the rational brain—is what makes us (think we are) so smart. Unlike the emotional brain, housed in the lymbic system, it knows you are no longer five when your mother criticizes and can tell the difference between your abusive father and your irritated partner. Its executive function is how you imagine a better future, make plans and decisions to fulfill it. PFC learning is affected throughout our lives; we are constantly adapting how we think with each positive and negative experience. Your brilliant PFC abilities shut down under threat: when you are emotionally triggered, the emotional brain takes control.

A trigger is a cue that reminds the traumatized emotional brain of the earlier event, which reacts as if it is happening again now. If you ever feel like you are losing your mind, you are actually only losing the half that can think clearly in a crisis. The stronger the emotion, the more it eclipses reason. Its unreasonable reactions are what you regret when you calm down and rational thoughts return. The solution to losing our mind is to keep the PFC active in the presence of a trigger so that it can remain in charge; this is essential self-regulation. Brain scans show the PFC lights up when we focus and concentrate. But intellect alone—PFC domination—can ignore self-preserving information in our animal instincts. Thoughts, ideas and beliefs can repress emotional information as when parents tell kids there's nothing to be afraid of and women are taught their anger is un-ladylike and therefore off limits. Overriding fear and anger leave us unprotected.

Meditation Is Self-Regulation

The solution to this battle of the brains is to get them to do their jobs in cooperation. Fortunately, you have an internal mediator: the "meditative mind," which is developed through the many practices of meditation. The meditative mind is able to be completely "present" to what is happening in real-time; it remains neutral to both triggers and trauma, while emotional brain conflates reality with memory and intellect may dwell on the future. This neutral position gives us the ability to weave instinct and intellect together for accurate assessment of a situation, using information from past experience with up-to-date intelligence to guide our actions. Meditation gives us access to all our brain's functions and proves to be a key to working with emotions to resolve reactive patterns and heal trauma. This is advanced/ skillful/next-level self-regulation!

The ability of the body and mind to regulate themselves was discovered long ago and developed into the various systems of yoga and meditation and now we have the science to prove their efficacy. It was truly a magnificent historical innovation to redirect the always outwardly-directed senses and attention—used to explore the world around us—and redirect them inward to explore the experiencer. The goal is to directly and personally understand the most important thing in your world—yourself.

Common to all meditative practices, the meditator is given one or more specific thing on which to focus, learning to hold the mind from wandering to other external stimuli and internal distractions and to bring the mind back to the intended focus when it strays away. We become the observer of experience, like sitting on the bank of a river instead of caught up in the rapids. You do the same when trying to write an important assignment, but meditation leaves the body calmer and the mind more peaceful afterward than does intellectual activity. Try this guided meditation in which imagination creates the object of focus and the images help manage the mind.

The Riverbank Meditation

Sit comfortably in a quiet place with eyes closed and breathe deeply for several minutes until you feel calm. Imagine a movie screen in your head and on it see yourself sitting on a flat, sunny riverbank at the edge of a wide and mighty river. The water is moving strong and steady from right to left in front of you, while you are safe and warm. Use all your senses to enjoy the beauty and yourself. In this serenity, you can notice thoughts in your head; see them floating on the river as they approach from your right, pass in front of you and then go on past to the left and disappear into the distance. Watch thoughts come and go; let them flow as you remain on the bank enjoying the scene.

Choose a particulary wonderful thought, something you love and want and watch it coming closer. As it passes in front, fully enjoy it. Then let it pass on by. Is it hard to let it go? Do you want to jump in the river, grab on, stay with it awhile? Forever? Imagine that's what happens when you obsess and crave and can't stop thinking about something you desire. Get back to the bank, sitting peacefully.

Now choose a disturbing thought, something recent or distant memory of pain, hatred, ugliness. Watch it come into your presence as it comes into your head sometimes. Watch yourself jump in again and hang on while you struggle to get free; but you are stuck and go way down the river together, you and your thoughts. Let it go and get out, back to the safe, warm, peaceful side of the river. Relax and watch. Follow another positive thought, less attached this time. Practice choosing to cling and follow, or watch thoughts come and go. You have the power to choose.

/ /

You must develop a relationship with your mind and its thoughts, a familiar and cooperative dialogue and make it clear that you, not your mind, is in charge. This is a skill gained and a goal of meditation. Visualizations are not for everyone. Some of us learn better with words and sounds, some are tactile learners. Body-centered awareness, beginning with feeling safe in one's body, is a key to working with trauma, with emotions and for healing our interconnected systems. Mindfulness is a meditation technique using senses and sensations to increase awareness.

Mindful Awareness Is Your Cure

Have you ever been to a rock concert where the music is so loud you can't hear the person next to you shouting in your ear? Similarly, communication from your total sensory system—sensations, thoughts, emotions—always let you know what you feel, what is wrong and what to do about it, but when the chaos, drama and the noise in your head are too loud, we don't hear. You know everything, you're just not aware. You can't change what you cannot see and feel. Mindfulness is a useful term and now a brand of meditation practices, that uses body-centered awareness to quickly re-awaken the ability to listen to inner wisdom. Be aware of the skin on your right hand right now. You feel that? Now, notice how you are breathing. Do you feel your belly moving, the coolness in your nose? That was happening the moment before, but it only dawned on your consciousness by directing your attention to it. In this same way you can know most everything about yourself. Try this quick mindfulness experience—even if you are an experienced meditator; it sets up the work with emotions to follow.

The Power of Paying Attention

You can read and follow each step, or listen here: www.emotional-liberation.com/resources. The best experience will be to record the script in your own soothing voice; do it on your phone right now!

Sit comfortably in a quiet place and close your eyes. Go slowly through these steps. Pay attention to every aspect of your breathing: sound, movement in the chest and sensation in the nose and throat. Breathe slowly with full but not strained inhalation and complete exhalation. This alone will help the mind toward calmness and clarity. Scan your body for any sensations, noticing and allowing all without stopping on any one. Let your body soften and relax, assisted by the breathing. Notice anything else your senses bring in. Ask your mind to relax with the body, take a break and just watch without "talking" in your head. Don't struggle: just invite and allow. Are there any emotional feelings in the body or felt more subtly? If so, feel and allow them. They are part of you, as important and needed as your heartbeat. Let the "observer" that is noticing and instructing watch your thoughts as well. Observe and allow, accept and let go. Now use this same process to look at or listen to your current life. Let awareness flow and bring you images and feelings about how things are going for you, how you feel about yourself and circumstances. This may begin to engage your emotions and get the thoughts going faster. As before, observe, accept and allow what is. Keep asking body and mind to relax as you review whatever presents itself as a problem or excitement. Go back to breath and body to know that you are present and okay. Move now to positive and pleasant thoughts and memories. Can you remain neutrally observing of them? Is it harder or easier to do so than with any troubling matters? Let all thoughts and focus go and come back to body and breath awareness once again. When you feel complete with this experience, slowly open your eyes. How do you feel? What did you find?

/ /

Practicing mindfulness develops our ability to observe objectively, accept more, judge less and therefore react less. In time, a gap between a stimulus and our responses becomes natural. We train the brain to act and not react. As mindfulness increases, losing your mind decreases. Develop the habit of listening to yourself and use it when confronted with anything difficult. What comes from that listening will be to see your way clearly through adversity and to deal with the thing. This is the power of the meditative mind.

Whole-System Healing

Trauma shocks us to the core and affects body, mind, emotions, behavior, beliefs and attitudes and the very spirit in us. All are set in a defensive posture, ready for the next blow. Healing trauma must therefore touch all aspects of our being as well. The work of Bessel van der Kolk, M.D., Peter Levine, PhD, Gabor Mate, M.D. and many others have proven the effectiveness—the necessity—of therapies that work with our whole system. EMDR helps post-traumatic stress disorder using eye movement to access memories and sensations that invoke the brain's natural healing powers. The system of Kundalini Yoga that I have practiced and taught for 40 years boasts a constant abundance of stories of healing. I was delighted to find in *The Body Keeps the Score*, that over that same period of time, Bessel van der Kolk was scientifically proving the benefits of yoga, rhythm and movement, singing and chanting that came to me through traditions from India. The shaking exercise in Chapter 2 is an example and dozens of practices can be found in my book, *Senses of the Soul*, where I go deeper into whole-system emotional healing work.

According to Sat Bir Khalsa, Ph.D. Asst. Prof. of Medicine, Harvard Medical School, research has shown that yoga practice enhances self-regulation of mental and emotional functioning and also increases mind-body awareness or mindfulness. Yoga practitioners become more aware of and sensitive to emotions while at the same time becoming less reactive to and driven by them.

"I've done a lot of therapy, but something about that movement made everything I've been dealing with clear for the first time." —Claire, in a kundalini class for emotions

Of all the complex parts of our being, emotions are the last frontier, a dark and dense jungle we have avoided. Yet they are always there, awaiting our understanding and cooperation. We are finding—you will find—our feelings are our friends. With better information, techniques and a healthy curiosity, we forge a new path to psychological healing and well-being in which you are the agent rather than the patient, not just having someone work on you, but also doing the work yourself. The responsibility and the power for our elevation lie within each of us.

Chapter 4

Emotions: Antibodies of Your Psychological Immune System

"From kindergarten onward, children should be taught about 'taking care of emotion.' Whether religious or not, as a human being we should learn more about our system of emotions so that we can tackle destructive emotion, in order to become more calm, have more inner peace." —The Dalai Lama, Time Magazine Interview, *March 18, 2019*

I agree with the Dalai Lama! Knowing how your amazing "system of emotions" works is the goal of this book. Your emotions rise only to tell you something: listening mindfully is the way to receive their help. Changing old perceptions and beliefs that Fear, Anger and the like are bad things to be avoided is a first step that will interest you in working with, rather than against, your feelings. As emotions researcher Susan David says, approach them with curiosity and compassion. You'd better work with them, because you cannot be rid of them. Emotions arise automatically in response to how things are going for you in this world. Troublesome feelings bring information and energy to avoid and correct disruptions to your happiness, while pleasant feelings tell you all is well.

My hope is that you will learn to work with your emotions so that they will not haunt you but rather help you find increasing levels of well-being. To change old misuse of emotions takes time, openness to experimentation and practice. With that investment, you will surely build trust in yourself and your feelings. In the chapters to come, I offer a carefully guided tour of the principal challenging emotions and their role in dealing with today and healing the after-effects of adverse life events. In this chapter, I will present the general case for emotions as essential catalysts for psychological wellness and how to use them as such.

My Search and Research

From the beginning, I was interested in how things work, taking them apart to see what was inside, just to know, or to fix and create something new. This led me to math and physics—how the universe works, but I soon realized I was more interested in how human lives work—or don't. I sought answers to my own problems and discoveries that would help people's inner worlds. After sampling spiritual and self-improvement approaches, I found yoga philosophy and practices—the ancient system of self-psychology—to satisfy my scientific mind. It is a system developed to solve the human condition with its "clinical trials" in addressing the human condition spanning thousands of years, millions of people and a vast body of self-reported benefits. While yoga in the West is used primarily for physical health, its original goal was to examine the causes of suffering and unhappiness. The yogic perspective is that our problems "out there" in the world are caused by and can best be resolved by working from the inside, the world of thoughts, feelings and spirit.

This approach and personal insight enhanced my ability to help others as a yoga therapist and counselor. After some time, I noticed a fascinating trend. People have all sorts of different issues, problems and challenges to overcome and each comes with strong "negative" emotions. One or more of just seven emotions were common to everyone's problems. That is, they are systematic. I began to ask why emotions are common factors in human suffering. Traditional thinking has been that emotions are a weakness, a character defect, a sin and a problem in themselves—the source of our troubles. A single clue from my teacher—"Emotions are the senses of the soul"— had me start looking at emotions as a source of valuable information, wisdom and healing. Just as our five physical senses navigate the physical world, our emotional feelings guide us through the complexities of how well life is going at the moment and overall. How you feel about something is a more subtle mix of qualities and conditions beyond temporary physical satisfaction. While your emotional state does not define happiness, it serves to guide you there and away from suffering.

I have found there to be just seven primary emotions that cause all the trouble we have with our feelings: Desire, Fear, Anger, Grief, Depression, Guilt and Shame. These are the "family names" of a group of related varieties and presentations of the core emotion. Throughout the book I capitalize the family name as a proper noun, as it most certainly deserves that respect. The same name appears in lowercase when describing a specific example and in stories where students use lowercase. Finding our way through the complex world of feelings and developing overall emotional fluency is greatly simplified with a focus on just these seven. Now, the story of how I discovered how our psychological self-healing system works.

Your Psychological Immune System

An emotional response to suffering is like the body's fever response to fighting an infection. Heat, swelling and pus are uncomfortable but not the real problem: they reveal and are attempts to heal, the underlying problem. I began to see emotions as that same kind of helpful response to environmental attacks on a person's quality of life. Emotions are not the problem but a healing-intended reaction that lets you know that some aspect of your well-being is challenged. Their discomfort brings attention to the real issue so it can be resolved. Emotions are the antibodies of your psychological immune system, always present to guide you to ever-improving well-being.

With a little guidance to accept and work with their feelings, my clients quickly find remarkably effective answers to and relief from their issues. And they can to do this process on their own, at their sage pace. Emotions are so systematic, so predictable in their cause and effect and so reliable in their solutions, that understanding and skilled use of emotion is, I claim, nature's own psychological healing system. Therefore, it needs to be integrated into all mental health therapies, trauma and addiction recovery programs and the successful processing of everyday challenges.

Skilled use of your emotional self-healing system can be learned and practiced. The first step has already begun: a change in perception and a shift in attitude toward emotions. They are not a nuisance, a weakness, or a problem to get rid of. Instead, emotions are a valuable resource in personal development, an essential element of our self-healing system. Your emotions are not a problem; they are part of a solution. They evolved along with our brain in the constant environment of challenge and change to help us cope and adapt. Traumas—adverse experiences and their effects—have been present throughout time. Our body/mind/spirit system evolved precise sensors and responses to the many dimensions of trauma, which we will detail in the emotion-specific chapters that follow.

Working with Evolution

It is a challenging task to train the ancient animal emotions within us. They are as automatic as a Trojan virus in your computer: once you open the email, the cascade of events is rapid and unstoppable. That virus—and your emotional reactions—are both algorithms, a chain of well-defined commands. An algorithm is a sequence of steps that is used to process numbers, situations, or problems to reach decisions and outcomes. In your emotional reactions, ancient algorithms involving thoughts, sensations and emotions, designed to solve primitive problems, are deciding your actions beyond your conscious control. You can't rewrite the underlying code of your instincts, but you can better manage nature's intent in writing these programs, which is always to help you to live.

Pesky Emotions Have a Positive Purpose

Emotions are automatic and situation-specific. In dangerous conditions, Fear appears, uninvited. Guilt comes to you in very different circumstances. In both cases, you much prefer not to feel that way. Relief from each uncomfortable emotion demands a price; it requires the initial conditions to change, to become more favorable to your well-being at some level. Fear requires that you create safety; when you do so, you enjoy peace. Guilt demands that you resolve a conflict of values and when you do, you can forgive and feel purity and innocence. Just as each emotion arises predictably, matched to your current issues, it also has a known purpose and outcome that completes its task. The result is not just relief from the uncomfortable emotion: it gives way to its pleasant-feeling partner. Shame melts into compassion, Anger is raised to grace and craving gives way to contentment. Think of them as the higher octave of the lower emotion, just as a low C note is somber compared to its brighter high C. The upgraded emotional states are like electrons making quantum leaps to outer "shells" surrounding an atom when they absorb energy. The jump to a condition that has more dynamic power.

Knowing how things work gives us the ability to work with them beneficially: that is how science leads to technology, which, when used wisely, improves the quality of life. The physics and statistical record of weather makes us able to predict it. Your emotions are at least as predictable and much more controllable than the weather. The correlation between the conditions that produce a specific emotion and what will relieve it is incredibly systematic and entirely predictable. The consistency of the human emotional response system gives us a powerful and accurate tool to diagnose psychological affect, understand their immediate and distant origins and prescribe solutions. It is a complete therapeutic approach that can be used by a therapist or for self-therapy. In any system, we need a shared vocabulary, the ability to name the symptoms we call feelings.

Emotional Literacy—Naming Felt Experiences

Emotion is a "felt experience": it happens inside you and can be as elusive to describe as attempting to explain color to a person without sight. To name a thing is essential to gather knowledge about it. Discussing feelings is already tricky enough socially, but you can change that. The ability to comfortably share how you feel—at the right time with the right people—is a gift to your emotional health. Very often, people can't name what they are feeling. As it is the first step in the SOS Method, you need to know the sensations associated with Shame as distinct from Guilt and from Grief apart from Depression. These two pairs are often mistaken one for the other, but their purpose and process are different: knowing which you are feeling makes for faster recovery. If you find you need more help with the particular markers of the emotions, that is covered in more detail in my book the *Senses of the Soul*.

Build your emotional vocabulary by spending some time with the list below. It is a combination of pure emotions and mental/emotional states or conditions associated with a feeling. The words are grouped under the seven principal family names addressed in this book, together with their varieties and manifestations. In the box to the right of these troubling emotions are their complements, not so much their opposites as their positive higher-octave states; these are the feelings that are produced by the proper channeling of the emotions on the left. This is an essential principle of emotional liberation: every troubling emotion has a higher purpose.

DESIRE	
Detrimental	Beneficial
Craving	Affection
Obsession	Interest/ Amusement
Addiction	Contentment
Envy	Curiosity/ Wonder
Greed	Longing
Jealousy	Euphoria/ Ecstasy
Lust	Empathy
Passion	Passion
Self-Deprivation	Enthusiasm
Scarcity Mentality	Pleasure/ Enjoyment
Negative Desires:	Gratification/Satisfaction
Dislike/ Revulsion	Joy/ Happiness

FEAR	
Detrimental	**Beneficial**
Worry	Safety
Insecurity	Security
Scared	Stability
Threatened	Relaxation
Angst	Ease
Anxiety	Focus
Distrust	Flow
Fright/ Horror	Awe
Terror/ Panic	Wonder
Suspicion	Trust
Intimidation	Confidence

ANGER	
Detrimental	**Beneficial**
Annoyance	Courage
Irritation	Generosity
Frustration	Protection
Contempt	Empowerment
Resentment	Control
Hostility	Effectiveness
Vengeance/ Wrath	Determination
Cruelty	Productivity
Hatred	Leadership
Rage	Accomplishment

GRIEF	
Detrimental	**Beneficial**
Anguish/ Sorrow	Thankfulness
Sadness/ Sorrow	Gratitude
Disappointment	Love

Regret	Reverence
Bereavement	Warmth of Heart
Suffering from Loss	Fullness of Heart
Loneliness	Kindness
Sympathy/ Pity	Caring

DEPRESSION	
Detrimental	**Beneficial**
Despair	Hope
Apathy	Optimism
Boredom	Willingness
Dejected	Motivation
Hopelessness	Purposefulness
Helplessness	Renewal
Powerlessness	Rebirth/ Rejuvenation

GUILT	
Detrimental	**Beneficial**
Remorse/ Regret	Truth
Accusation/ Blame	Trust
Punishment	Integrity
Wickedness	Honesty
Conflicted Values	Forgiveness
Violated Morals	Innocence
Confused Ethics	Purity

SHAME	
Detrimental	**Beneficial**
Rejection	Acceptance
Abandonment	Pride
Abuse - Neglect	Allowing
Embarrassment	Dignity/ Respect
Humiliation	Humility

Inadequacy	Compassion
Pity/ Scorn	Self-Love
Worthlessness	Love/ Sacredness
Shyness	Self-confidence
Not Enough-ness	Social connection

Losing Your Mind—Emotions Unused and Misused

With a vocabulary and an understanding of the functional value of emotions—what they are—we are in a position to let them help us. People always had an immune system, but until science understood how it works, our ignorance of hygiene caused illnesses we no longer suffer from. To emerge from these emotional dark ages, we bring together what we know about how the brain is affected by emotion and meditation to show *how to use them* skillfully to improve rather than ruin our lives. We all have lots of experience in how NOT to use emotions.

Unbridled expression of emotion is the thing that gives feelings their unintended consequences and a bad reputation. When you react impulsively without input from the executive function of your frontal brain, the animal instincts of your emotional brain take over and you lose control. Over-reacting is like an automatic fire sprinkler system flooding your house over burnt toast.

Repression is the polar opposite misuse of emotion. This strategy—to not feel or to control emotions—is taught by parents, religions and all who want to avoid your and their uncomfortable feelings and bad behaviors. Will-powered attempts to overcome emotion do keep society from falling apart—we can behave ourselves—but they also lead to denial, inauthenticity, disassociation from one's own reality and numbness. Feelings that are ignored and blocked but later explode in open or secretive abuse is a tragic but typical example. In repression, the prefrontal cortex maintains a belief that overrides and suppresses the limbic system's emotional response, at the cost of vital instinctual information the emotional brain contains.

Keeping Your Head

The solution is to keep the frontal lobe active and in conscious awareness during emotional activation. Because it can tell the difference between what is happening now and an older crisis, your responses and solutions benefit from all you are capable of today; your earlier, traumatized self is not in charge. How to use both simultaneously? Mind focusing activities, like meditation, turn on the PFC and uncomfortable thoughts, like painful memories and future fears, awaken the limbic system. Bring troubling memories to mind while you are mindful; use the clarity of your meditative mind to gain emotional intelligence. The various techniques in this book employ this basic approach: to create clarity and maintain it while inviting emotion to rise by recalling the thoughts, memories and issues that upset us. You can then observe and learn from them without becoming lost or overwhelmed. Use anything that gets you to clarity: walking silently in the woods or lying in bed, not daydreaming or mind-wandering, but being completely aware of the present moment. That is the condition in which to do emotional healing.

"If you can keep your head when all about you are losing theirs...Yours is the earth and everything that's in it." —from If *by Rudyard Kipling*

A Method for Our Madness

When intellect and emotion are co-active, we more quickly

realize solutions to the disturbances that emotions are detecting. We can ask questions like, "What will make me feel better?" and, "How can I solve this problem?" and receive answers that are not limited to our narrow field of existing beliefs and earlier experiences, nor controlled by a traumatized brain. This requires a retraining in how we listen for answers which we learned to get from thoughts in the mind, a way so foreign to most people we struggle to describe it. "I felt the answer in my belly." "My heart spoke." "I saw my solution like a movie." "It said, 'Don't worry, just love yourself.'" "It was an instant knowing, without words." "My soul said..." These are descriptions I hear from people all the time when using this technique. They sound like "God spoke," and "the still, small voice" heard by prophets of old. As with them, you won't readily trust these voices until you try following their guidance and gather proof that it is the truth.

This shift takes time; it is different from how we learned to function primarily from the left side of the brain to analyze and decide things. Any complex ability is best learned progressively from simple steps repeated in controlled conditions to more challenging situations later on. You learn to drive on empty streets with a teacher before taking on the freeway and play scales on piano long before a concert performance. Just so, emotional skills are gained with guidance and quiet practice before you can expect to keep your cool and respond optimally in a situation that would have previously caused you to "lose your mind."

The SOS Method: Simple Steps for Working with Emotions

This is both a set of instructions and a guided meditation. Read through it once for comprehension. Then go through the steps meditatively. Record a version of this, leaving out some explanation in favor of speaking guidance directly to you inner activity and use that to lead you through the steps.

1. Focus and Feel. Ask, "What Am I Feeling?"

We begin by allowing, rather than resisting, emotion. Sit quietly in a place where you can relax and focus. Approach your practice with curiosity and a purpose of discovery. Spend several minutes creating calmness and clarity so you can observe your thoughts and feelings, unlike during real-time upsets when they overpower you. Use anything that increases your clarity and safety: exercise, yoga, meditation, calming music and the assistance of live or recorded guidance for example: Breathe long, deep, full breaths for several minutes. Take in all physical, mental and emotional sensations without "thinking" about them; just experience them directly without comment.

When you feel ready to invite in your feelings by emotions, recall any troubling situation or painful memory—anything that bothers you will trigger the emotion. How deep you go is your choice; start with a smaller issue. Vividly relive that memory—you will feel the same emotions now that you did before. Allow and observe them. Let yourself fully feel the bodily sensations. They may be unpleasant but they won't hurt you. Think of them as similar to getting into a hot tub: it is uncomfortable at first, but you know it will be good for you, so you slowly get used to the feelings. Where in your body are the sensations? Does it feel tight, tingly, hot or cold, dark and congested? Discomfort is how they get your attention and speak—they use information-packed feelings rather than words. Let it be without resistence.

A first goal is to no longer be intimidated by emotional feelings. Your feelings are nothing to be afraid of; allow them to pass through you; you can handle them. As you relax into them, the intensity softens. You need some degree of ease to be in dialogue with them in the next step. Some will feel nothing, usually when repression has been the habit. And if it is overwhelming or re-triggering, just stop and engage in some physical activity to help the emotions pass.

Can you name the emotion(s) you are feeling? Just as naming a disease facilitates and directs the treatment, identifying your emotions leads you to its unique purpose. Familiarity with the Emotional Intelligence Guide in Chapter 4 will help. The inability to name what one is feeling is quite common. Watch for terms like, "I feel...betrayed, abused, lost, alone" which are situations and thoughts. How do you feel about those things? Relate feelings to their family name. For example, confused, anxious, worried and panic are all Fear. If you name more than one emotion, choose to address just one at a time—perhaps the strongest or most familiar.

2. Find the Source. Ask, "Why am I Feeling This?"

Once you can remain cognitively present while feeling the emotion, you can have two-way communication with it. Relax your thinking mind so it can quietly observe answers that come more from your body than in the form of thoughts. Imagine the emotion you have named is a helpful presence and voice you can converse with. Ask it, "Why are you here? What is wrong that summoned you?" Get to the root of the problem with questions like, "Why is that a problem for me?"

Learn to listen with your entire being. An answer may come instantly, seemingly from nowhere and without "thinking." Some people hear words while others feel the replies as an instant knowingness or see images that have meaning to them. Learning your way of accessing wisdom is part of the process. Ask and then be open to what comes without trying to find an answer. It may take a bit of practice to hear this subtle message directly before the mind steps in to analyze, judge, deny or reject the message. Trust what you hear and feel, even if it doesn't make sense right away. Once you discover this way of knowing, you can ask any question.

3. Find the Solution. Ask, "What Do I Need to Feel Better?"

Once you understand what's disturbing you, ask your emotions what they need for things to be right: "What must I know or do to feel better? "My Fear (or whichever emotion is presenting), what do you want?" "How can I help you bring me to peace?" If the answer is not clear, ask again.

When solutions are sought, the mind will be eager to help; hold it off in its observing role. Use your mind's eye to envision any solutions you receive; try several and play them out. This is where intuition can bring amazingly accurate answers beyond what you have believed or tried. When you get a response, your mind may resist and begin to rationalize away something new and untested. Don't engage in a debate, simply take in whatever you experience.

//

Learning to hear that quiet voice is part of the training, so, if it is not immediately apparent, keep trying. Remember these solutions, whether or not they make sense and whether or not you think you can (or will) do them. Remember to listen first: ask the mind to wait to analyze and assist with a strategy, even if just seconds after the answers come. You will see that these amazingly accurate answers come from a place of higher knowledge than your mind's thinking can access.

4. Take Action. How Will You Implement These Answers?

Now it's the mind's turn to help with on-the-ground logistics of implementing these intuitive answers. Act on the needs and solutions you've gathered to resolve the situation.

Remember Alice's story at the beginning of the book? Review it now to see how she followed this sequence with this last step remaining to do after our session. Your path to feeling better may require a single task or communication, or it might take years to accomplish. Either way, you will feel better just knowing what is needed to move toward resolution. Rather than actions, your solutions may be new truths, attitudes and guiding principles like, "I am worthy of love." While you may have heard these things before in books, they have a more profound meaning and impact coming from within yourself.

You will feel better! You will begin to feel better immediately, in Step 1, because the emotions back off a bit when they have succeeded in getting your attention. You will feel a little better again in Steps 2 and 3 as the feelings deliver their message. The downside of this immediate relief is that beginning to feel better can diminish the impetus to take action. But without completing this last step, the emotions will return until you do. A lasting improvement in your feelings regarding this situation indicates that your corrections are working.

5. Review and Repeat

In any one session, you may not hear answers, but each experience is valuable and builds both skills and self-knowledge toward ultimate healing. Continue this process whenever feelings arise and continually create the improvements you require.

Take time to write down what you experienced and learned after each session. What did you learn about yourself;

about the situation? Did you get solutions? What did you learn about how to work with emotions? Does some of the previous information in this book make more sense in light of your experience? Can you begin to see some value in your feelings?

Replacing old patterns takes time and focus. Just as solving a puzzle happens piece by piece, solutions to challenges and emotional upsets come in steps. Take whatever clarity comes to you in one session as the starting point of your next inquiry. Your source of inner answers is available anytime you tap in.

Emotional Intelligence Guide			
Emotion	Source	Solution	Transformation
Fear Excitement, Doubt, Indecision, Worry, Confusion, Overwhelm, Anxiety, Panic, Terror	Threat Danger	Survival Safety Security Stability	Relaxation Peace Confidence Fearlessness
Desire Longing, Yearning, Craving, Obsession, Addiction (and opposites: Aversion, Repulsion)	Needs Wants	Gratification Satisfaction Enjoyment Contentment	Joy Fulfillment Serenity Desirelessness

Anger Bothered, Irritation, Frustration, Blame, Resentment, Fury, Rage	Harm Over-Powered Loss of Control Disrespect	Protection Determination Control Management	Empowerment Honor Grace
Depression Boredom, Discouragement, Desperation, Despair, Despondency, Apathy, Helplessness, Hopelessness	Dysfunction Need for Change Exhausted Resources	Surrender Release Renewal Revitalization	Willingness Optimism Hope
Grief Sadness, Sorrow, Loneliness	Loss Longing Change	Letting Go of What Was Embracing What Is Completion Appreciation	Love Reverence Wholeness Self-Actualization
Guilt Regret, Remorse	Mistakes Lessons to Learn Conflicted Values Confused Ethics	Values Examination Truth-Telling Taking Responsibility Forgiveness	Integrity Trust Innocence Neutrality
Shame Embarassment, Humiliation, Perfectionism, Disgust, Not-Enoughness, Self-Loathing	Abuse/ Neglect Rejection Abandonment Low Self-Worth	Acceptance Loving-Kindness Compassion	Self-Love Tolerance Transcendence

Decoding the Seven Difficult Emotions' Purpose

In my work with clients, I found that that one or more of the seven emotions presented here are felt whenever there is a problem. While each has a family of variations and intensities, they are like the three primary colors from which all other colors are mixtures. Feelings are complex and many, but easier to understand when working with one distinct actor at a time. Science separates complicated systems into elements: examining one at a time helps to more easily understand the whole. We can do the same: take on our swirling feelings one pure element at a time.

For example, Jealousy is a combination of Desire, Anger and Depression (Apathy). I want something, feel powerless to get it and am mad at you for having what I want. There might be a touch of Shame involved if I don't feel I deserve it. I am more likely to understand and resolve my jealousy, if I can separate and work with these one at a time. Desire will help me clarify exactly what it is that I want. Depression and/or Shame can help me understand why I think I can't have it and redirect my efforts. And Anger well directed will give me the power to take action and get it.

Refer to the Emotional Intelligence Guide, which distills the fundamental cause and purpose of these primary emotions. It serves as a map to help you find answers to the SOS Method's four questions. For example, I am anxious about dating, or a big disagreement I'm having with my partner. For the first question, "What am I feeling?" I identify anxiety in the first column to be a form of Fear. To answer, "Why am I feeling Fear?" I go beyond my ususal, "I don't know why," or "Because of the fight." Column two shows Fear will always arise in response to some danger or threat to my well-being, real or imagined. So, I ask, "How does conflict with my wife threaten me? She might take away any of the many things I need from her: attention, affection, meals, she might leave me altogether. Each of those threatens a specific aspect of my health and happiness."

To get started on solutions to the third question—"What do I need to feel better?"—column three shows that Fear's purpose is to keep me safe and secure. So, I look to solutions that will do so. I could overcome my habit to withdraw and go work it out with her. I can humble myself and apologize, though I never have before. I could ask the hard questions, "Are you going to leave me over this?" or "What will it take to make up?" I could also make internal changes, examining my own lack of trust in fearing that our relationship cannot weather a serious disagreement.

This intelligent analysis can go a long way toward resolving issues and thereby quieting emotions that arise to alert you of the problem. At the same time, these solutions are limited by all that has been thought and tried before: the traumatized brain and our socialized habits will look to old ways that haven't worked. That is why applying the meditative mind to answer the questions from the openness of the neutral mind is essential to find innovative answers. Analysis by the PFC and intuition of a well-mangaged limbic system (emotional brain) is again using the two in sync. It's also a thrill for me when people confirm answers from their meditations—"I will no longer be controlled by him"—from their mindful work with Anger and then find on the Guide that Anger has to do with control issues.

The fourth step is to implement information gathered under the domain of the brain's executive functioning. You may find yourself reluctant to try new things like speaking up as never before, even though it felt so good to imagine finally doing so. This is the process of developing trust in yourself, in your emotions as truthtellers.

The Dance of Emotions, Trauma and Triggers

In your earliest traumas, including prenatal experiences, Fear was there to warn, Anger rose to protect and Grief came to console. But you weren't capable of using them. Emotions never quit trying to help you in present-day upsets and they are still working to heal past wounds. When they are fully discharged in the successful handling of an adverse experience, you return to equilibrium. The takeaway is trust in the emotion and greater confidence to handle similar situations: positive personal development. With trauma, especially early in life, you have little ability and scarce guidance to use your emotions well. When they are called into action but can't be used—we are often told what to feel or not, treated worse for our feelings, or left to suffer alone with them—they don't disappear. They remain vigilant, waiting for a time they might succeed. Meanwhile, we are imprinted with diminished safety, self-confidence and emotional balance. Example:

> I was overpowered and abused; Anger couldn't protect me. It boiled deep inside me but on the outside, I was scared and defeated. That heat builds and finds unrelated outlets: I'm mean to my friends or have none. I fantasize about harming others. I misbehave and begin cutting or rebellious drug and sex use. Repression alternates with lashing out. Anger is misdirected from protection to destruction, embedded in automatic reactions. Anger, flailing to help me, is easily unleashed by my unique triggers. Anger is now hijacked and locked into a dysfunctional misuse that doesn't fulfill its mission. Harm continues by my inaction or by my own hand. Anger, always responding to

harm, increases. The unrequited earlier abuse is conflated with my current situation of harm; I can't handle today and the past still hurts. How to break the cycle?

Past and present are indistinguishable to the emotional brain and we can use that to heal the past and handle the present. The two share the same lessons and skills; what I needed then I also need now. I work with Anger to better handle present-day situations that trigger me. I also explore past harm to find what would have saved me or at least made it better. Most often, the solutions are the same. Continuing the example:

> In a mindful state I realize I need to finally take control of my life, which went off the rails long ago. I'll stop blaming everyone and start getting myself together. I can't control everything that happens but I can do my best and keep going. I need to speak up when people hurt me, set boundaries or get away from toxic relationships as soon as I can. I can get help with what I can't handle. Those same truths would have helped when I was hurt before. I now know my power to deal with something like that today, so I can trust myself, relax any hyper-vigilance, feel confident and comfortable.

Recall our definition of and metric for trauma healing: "When I have grown to know now what I didn't know then, when I can do now what I couldn't do then, to handle and make similar situations okay now that weren't okay then, I have learned the lesson for which my soul brought that trauma and I am healed."

In the exercise to follow, use the thoughts and memories of your triggered-state pattern as the emotional prompt. Reviewing that past event will give insight that, when applied, alters your future response to the same situation. Just so, memories and feelings of very early trauma can be reviewed and possible solutions to that earlier situation discovered. Your subconscious protections want to know how to avoid similar pain in the future. This will accomplish the growth and enhanced behavior that will provide a sense of safety that was previously unavailable and may have been missing ever since. When you see a solution from your present consciousness that was impossible to know or do back then and can apply it to similar challenges now, your emotional guides have fulfilled their purpose. The lesson is learned, the issue resolved and the emotions subside.

///

Put Emotions to Work

Put together all you know from your patterns worksheet and the Emotional Intelligence Guide to use your meditative mind with the SOS Method using these brief cues in a self-therapy session. You might like to be guided through the process, which you can do using the audio here: www.emotional-liberation.com/resources.

Prepare. Sit still, breathe deeply, focus on sensations without mental comments. Feel and answer from your body:

What am I feeling?

Why am I feeling it?

What do I need to feel better?

When you decide you are finished with this session, bring your awareness back in the here and now, take a few deep breaths and slowly open your eyes. I suggest that you make some notes of your experience as you might in learning any topic: here, your life and happiness is the subject.

It often takes many sessions to get all the answers, but they are available to probe at any time. Real progress comes from putting all that you learn from your emotional intelligence into practice. A message can be clear and accurate but take years to become a change in your life. And from that time on, you will enjoy the benefits of your efforts for a lifetime.

On your journey and in your emotional self-healing sessions, start with more recent and smaller issues, especially if you have any concerns about re-triggering significant trauma. Your emotions will bring up and invite you to deal with things when you are ready. That time has come! You have a chance now to use Anger to find your power and set boundaries, feel Grief to heal your heart, embrace Shame to accept and love yourself.

Dive In to Your Emotional Well-Being

Did you know far more of Earth's biomass is subterranean than is the life we see above ground? It is the same with your consciousness: more of what affects your life goes on mostly hidden, unexamined. Just as scientists explore deep caves to understand Earth, you can go spelunking in the fascinating depths of your own psychology to understand how to live well and happily. You are equipped for emotional cave-diving, in part with this book as a map and self-awareness to light the way. There are known paths to follow, discovered by brain scientists, trauma researchers, therapists, meditators and all who have come before you seeking relief. With safety from steady skill-building, openness to what you will find and optimism for a healthier life, you are ready to create emotional intelligence, emotional agility, emotional liberation. Getting to know how these emotions work and how to work with them is a fundamental study every human being needs.

Part Two:
Working with Emotions for Recovery and Beyond

Chapter 5

Regain Contentment: Use Desire to Get What You Need

You are so needy! But don't be embarrassed by it, everyone is. We need a million physical things to be alive and a million more psychological conditions to thrive. The difference between desperate neediness and well-adjusted confidence is your ability to feed your needs. Desire is the emotion that tells you what you want and it packs tremendous energy to go after it all. From finding food or a mate to finding a purpose in life, Desire will have you break rules, hearts and bodies to get what you want. You know the language of Desire: I like it, I love it, I want it, I gotta have it, I can't live without it. Fantasy, longing, obsessing and those feelings in your body: hunger, heat, pulling and pushing, lust, craving.

You also know that power is difficult to control. There are countless laws, rules and morals, diets and tools to help you do so, many who fear and want to control your desires. You may fear your desires and feel out of control. Personal restraint, willpower and discipline don't always work. As with all problematic emotions that threaten to overpower, we can either succumb to whatever Desire demands, or try to deny and repress it. Neither way works. Our approach will be to manage emotions by working with them to accomplish their essential purpose. Desire's purpose is to guide you from dissatisfaction to contentment. With it, you can make peace with the constant wanting that is our human condition.

If denying desire has ever worked to reach desirelessness, it certainly doesn't work for our culture today. Think you can discipline your desires? Just hold your breath and try talking yourself out of your need for air. Instead, learn to use this emotion for true self-care. This requires that you accurately discern what you truly need and consciously guide those wild horses through the fog of Desire to reach contentment. There is no happiness without it.

What Do I Want?

> *"I've been stuck so long between the fear of indecision and not knowing what I want on the one hand and the anger of not getting what I need on the other. As a child, I couldn't ask for anything; then I lost touch entirely with what I need. Working with desire one day, I realized I could just ask myself, 'What do I want?' I didn't know I have to figure out what I want if I'm ever going to get it. It took a while to get back in touch with my needs. I guess I thought I just automatically knew. Now, I have to learn how to speak up and ask. Why is that so scary? I was the youngest with four big brothers, so I guess I got used to there being nothing left for me. And my stressed-out parents got mad when I would ask for anything. It was safer to go without." —Jamila*

As Jamila discovered, a satisfying life requires the ability to identify what you need and then use the energy of Desire through your words and actions to get it. Beneath every upset is a need unmet. Think about any time you were ever mad, sad, scared, lonely, embarrassed, tired, aggressive, controlling, or shut down—what was it you wanted and weren't getting? Can you name the thing: food, sex, money, sleep, a friend, or a new toy? Or was it something non-physical: attention, security, love, freedom from being controlled, reaching a goal you valued? It is a parent's job to figure out what a crying infant needs and when they guess correctly and give it to the baby, peace returns. Are you so different? The skillful use of Desire will bring you that peace.

Further Understanding

An effort to fulfill a need is behind everything you do. Yes, we are all selfish; we want to survive and then thrive. Even to help and serve others selflessly fulfills the good feeling you get from doing so. That's all we are doing here on earth, so why aren't humans happy? We are unhappy in proportion to how poorly we work with our desires. As with all these heavy emotions, there are two ways Desire's purpose of bringing contentment leads to suffering instead. Too much Desire and indulgence in it makes us a slave to insatiable cravings, chronic dissatisfaction, unfulfilled efforts, addictions and binges. They feel so much bigger than you; you may feel small and helpless before them. Too little Desire leaves us empty or living life without flavor, fun, or pleasure. Relentless desires and the experiences of getting too much or not getting enough shapes us all. Needing is traumatic.

Connection to Trauma

Getting what you need has been a life-and-death issue from the moment of your conception. Going without can be—or certainly may seem to be—life-threatening and therefore traumatizing. We can say with confidence that every past trauma and every present-day trigger is the result of and a reaction to, the real or perceived lack of something vital to your physical, mental, or emotional well-being. More simply: Every trauma is a need blocked.

Every blocked need creates a reaction.

And current reactive patterns are dysfunctional attempts to obtain the same needs that were previously blocked, creating trauma. Therefore, reclaiming our natural ability to know what we need and get it—the skillful use of Desire—is essential to trauma recovery and a fulfilled life.

A Need Thwarted Becomes a Need Distorted

You may not remember how scary it was as a baby to need food, a clean diaper, or your mother's touch to feel safe. But when these essential things were not forthcoming and you had no way to get them for yourself, the unmet need created fear, anger, sadness, or other emotions. Not even the best parents were always there and knowing what you needed, so we all experienced the emptiness and insecurity of lack. And for many, the abuse was much more direct, the neglect much less benign. When the able-bodied caregivers that we biologically expect to help us survive are absent or turn against us, it is deeply traumatizing. We react with immediate physical pain and intense emotional response. And the trauma leaves us changed in ways that may last a lifetime. We acquire beliefs to help our young minds explain why we can't get what we need, whether it will ever be possible and how to adapt to that "reality." When we experience lack, it creates survival-level behavior patterns that begin to determine what we get in the future.

In Jamila's story above, un-attentive parents and older brothers left her frequently wanting. While far from starving, her mild but chronic deprivation created the effect of not expecting much, to the point of not asking for or even knowing what she needed. To lock this in, as the only girl, she was expected to fill in for her working mother—she was taught to ignore her needs and take care of others first. The imprinted belief that ran her life for 40 years was, "attending to the needs of others is how it works here and what I must do to survive." Her need to survive was fulfilled, but so many other needs for a satisfying life were not. Learning to work with her emotions, she sat quietly and listened to her body and the messages in her feelings. She began to get in touch with the pain of unfulfilled needs underlying the anger and sadness of not taking care of herself. Breaking the old beliefs that survival meant ignoring herself and attending to others, she started making time for herself to rest and enjoy simple things, saying "no" to unfair demands and disrespect and asserting her value at work.

Trauma never destroys your ability to know what you need and take care of yourself: it becomes clouded by survival-based coping strategies. Recovery from trauma includes reclaiming the ability to understand what you need accurately. That can be accessed anytime one can bypass the mind's traumatically imprinted machinations and listen directly to "intuitive instinct," meaning emotion interpreted through the intellect. This ability is the overall intention of this book and you will practice it with all seven emotions.

If we modify our definition and measure of trauma recovery with this idea that the basis of trauma is a disruption to getting what you need, it states:

When I now know and can adequately get what I need, which I didn't get at the time I was traumatized, I begin to relax and feel safe, which I did not feel then. I am healing.

Let's check the functioning of your innate ability to always know what you need. If it is blocked for any reason, practice can awaken it.

///

Feel the Desire to Know Your Need

Read through these instructions, then begin. You may need to open your eyes and read the next cue at any time.

Sit comfortably in a quiet place where you will not be disturbed. Set a timer for six minutes and close your eyes. Breathe in through puckered lips and exhale through your nose with a soft hmmm sound. Focus on your lips, which are so sensitive to feel the cool air. You use them for pleasures like kissing and tasting, which will connect you to Desire. Listen to the intimate whisper of the wh-oooooo sound of your inhale and that universal sound of satisfaction as you exhale. These sounds fill your body and connect you to pleasure. Can you enjoy those feelings, or do they bring discomfort, any bad feelings, or seem foreign to you? Keeping going and use all the sensations to relax into and explore your relationship to Desire.

As you continue the breath pattern, recall any memory in which you were upset, hurt, angry, scared, sad, or depressed. Feel now how you felt then. Breathe through those feelings and go deeper into your body. Be kind, understanding and generous. Be private and intimate with yourself. Ask your body what it needs. Feel the answer. Ask your heart, "What do you need?"

Don't think. Don't doubt, judge, or question. Learn to listen deeply.

Now imagine having all that you want of what you find that you need. How would you feel and act then? How would you like to go about getting it? When the time is up, keep going for as long as you like. When you slowly open your eyes, write down whatever you found.

///

The Wild World of Needs

"...Children have emotional needs and their mental and physical health depends as much on providing for these needs as on food, shelter and medicines...Mammals can't live on food alone. They need emotional bonds too." —Yuval Noah Harari, Homo Deus

You need food, warmth and shelter, and a working body to survive. Beyond those survival needs lie countless mental/emotional experiences we seek to go beyond merely existing: call them psychological needs. They make human lives incredibly more complicated and can even work against survival. To eat can gratify your hunger, but a satisfying meal is a richer experience. But then, are you content with your relationship with food and your body? And can food alone bring you fulfillment in life? And is there something beyond that—enlightenment? This sequence is a spectrum of human experience that begins with purely physical things and moves deeper into our innermost being. Realizing what you truly need at all levels—the motivations behind all your actions— and then acting to meet those needs is key to your personal peace and our global survival. We start by identifying those motivations that may be hidden or counterproductive.

A Few Common Needs

It's incredible that beyond basic survival, we do everything for the experience, the feeling it gives us. The first column of the following table contains things you do, behaviors. The second column are things you want to receive from others. You may be doing the first to get the second. The third column is how you want to feel and the ultimate goal and reason for all the rest. They are arranged in some common sequences for you to see how they work from outer actions to inner experiences.

You have any number of these needs; add any that you realize by reading them. Circle any that you recognize, first individually and separately, then in any mix-and-match combinations. Draw lines connecting your own sequences: I do X to get Y so I can feel Z.

Needs List		
What I Do	What I Want from Others	How I Want to Feel
I need to be in Control	to get Order	so I feel Safe
I need to be Productive	to get Praise	so I feel Worthy/Valuable
I need to be Perfect	to get Approval	so I feel Accepted
I need to be Right	to get Validation	so I feel Important
I need to Win/Achieve	to get Respect	so I feel Understood
I need to Give to Others	to get Appreciation	so I feel Loved
I need to be Nice/Conform	to get Acceptance	so I feel Harmony

What I Do	What I Want from Others	How I Want to Feel
I need to Look Good	to get Attention	so I feel Wanted
I need to Do It Myself	to get Independence	so I feel Confidence
I need to Please Others	to get Kindness	so I feel at Peace
I need to be Busy	to get Things	so I feel Alive
I need to be Responsible	to get people's Trust	so I feel Needed
I need to Have My Space	to get Left Alone	so I feel Free
I need to Have Sex	to get Tenderness	so I feel Connected
I need to Lead or Teach	to get Inspiration	so I feel Elevated
I need to Suffer	to get Help	so I feel Supported
I need to Confront/Argue	to get Energized	so I feel Powerful
I need to Hide/Not Speak	to get Agreement	so I feel Secure
I need to be Productive	to get Results	so I feel I am Needed
I need to be in Turmoil	to get Sympathy	so I feel I Belong
I need to Take Care of Others	to get Recognition	so I feel I have a Purpose

Can you see that these drive a great deal of your daily life and explain a lot of your emotional reactions? Notice that the first actions in the first column take a lot of work; they may not always be available to you and may not lead to what you are trying to get out of them. Sex may not be possible nor lead to tenderness. People may not recognize your efforts to caretake them nor appreciate all that you give.

Notice that you can receive things in the middle column in other ways. You could get energized from praising others and working together, ask for help directly without suffering and gain respect for kindness and cooperation rather than by beating others in competition.

Finally, notice that the inner experiences in the third column need not be dependent on any single strategy or source; there are unlimited ways to achieve feelings of security and connection. The meditation near the end of the chapter will help you further recognize needs and expand your sources and strategies so you can spend more time content and fulfilled. Now let's connect these underlying needs to your triggers and patterns.

Gettin' Cranky?

A sure way to better take care of yourself is to recognize when you are *not* happy about what you are getting. Every upset is a need not met. In your day-to-day life, what disturbs your peace and why? We all have common dissatisfaction reactions that I politely call "crankiness." Recognizing your particular way of getting cranky will help you catch and correct your needs deficits. How does your lousy mood look? Sullen, withdrawn and isolated? Critical, argumentative, bossy and angry? Sad, despairing, giving up, depressed? Hyperactive and busy? Over-doing your favorite go-to indulgence? If you don't know, ask someone who knows you well. They happen often enough to recall now and see them clearly.

Review a recurring upset, perhaps one of the emotional and behavioral reactive patterns explored earlier. Go back now and take a fresh look at the "needs and beliefs" sections of your reactions worksheet from Chapter 1. Ask, "Why do I start feeling disturbed?" What would solve it, bring relief and have me feeling fine again? What do I need to be happy?" Imagine you have one all-powerful wish that can bring you anything, make anything happen. What is your dream? Here's your chance to name it. Don't be practical. No excuses now for your suffering. Imagine getting that and how you feel with it. You can't always get what you want—when or exactly how you want it—but you can always find a way to get what you most need.

Working with Desire, you will become more aware of the needs that are common to both your patterns and the traumas that caused them. And with the help of all seven heavy emotions, you will find that you can break old habits that cause you to live in scarcity and discontentment. Think now, at the time of any emotional upset you care to recall, did you know what you needed to have remained calm and content? Did you get it?

Remember that earlier trauma-formed beliefs and coping strategies are at play in your current reactions. Here is a Desire-based adaptation of our trauma recovery statement applied to triggers:

> **When I understand and can adequately get what I need, I no longer react to situations that used to trigger me. When I come to trust that I can take care of myself now, which I was not able to do then, I feel secure. I have healed trauma-formed insecurities.**

Can you begin to see that beneath every upset is a need unmet? When you react emotionally, there is something you need and aren't getting. In the reactive state of mind, emotions overtake reason and your ability to fulfill the need diminishes. The need remains unmet; you remain upset and living in lack can become a habit. Likewise, when you get what you (really) need, you are not upset. If that were as easy as it sounds, we would all be getting along just fine.

How Satisfaction Goes Sideways

Why doesn't everyone always know what they want and be satisfied with what they can get? Why do we starve ourselves and overeat? Why do we long for love then fight, separate and feel lonely? Why do we obsess and become addicted to pleasurable things until they are killing us? We binge and horde. For animals, it is more straightforward: they fulfill their needs if the source is available. Our cognitive function gives us great flexibility and more resources to get what is not readily available; we can plan, strategize and create new ways to satisfy. Horses eat what is there; we make hundreds of flavors of ice cream, millions of restaurants. Birds mate; we have the Kama Sutra and sex toys. And still, we always want more; we tend to be discontent. How does it start? Here are a few of the many ways Desire's simple task to seek and satisfy goes off track. Mark all that you recognize.

> *"We were quite poor, growing up. It was just normal, so I never expected or tried for more."* (Experiences define what is possible and that becomes habitual.)

> *"My father caught a boy kissing me and called me a slut. Ever since, I feel guilty about sex."* (Socialization. Messages from others override our natural needs.)

> *"I never wanted anything but to be a therapist.*

122

I thought that wasn't macho enough, so I went into business; been miserable ever since." (Judging and abandoning true desires.)

"My needs? I had to take care of my family and was shamed for being selfish if I wanted something for myself. My dreams shut down long ago." (Your needs hijacked by others to fulfill their own. She was trained to give; lost touch with her own needs.)

"It's too scary asking for anything. Makes me feel vulnerable. What if they say 'no'?" (Needing is a weakness.)

"I'm lonely, but dating is so painful. I just watch porn instead." (Substitution with something that doesn't satisfy the real need; in this case, love and connection.)

"It's hard to ask for what I want; I don't feel I deserve to get or be happy." (Shame, low self-esteem.)

"My father was religious, serious and stern. He said laughter was frivolous and fun indulgent, that we should just work hard and do right." (Told what to want. Desiring is made to be altogether wrong.)

"I suppressed what I needed for 40 years with alcohol." (Numbing the pain of dissatisfaction instead of dealing with needs.)

To get Desire working, it is essential to understand your

relationship to it and how you got there, which will help free you from dysfunction. Reflect on your history with these questions.

How have desires been received, judged, feared, thwarted, or enjoyed and satisfied at different times in your life?

What beliefs did you hear and adopt or rebel from regarding pleasure and fun?

What do you feel you deserve and can expect?

How much does it take to be happy?

How easy or difficult is it to get what you want?

Are you more comfortable giving than receiving?

How do you feel about people who have more than you? Those who are poorer?

These are all just thoughts that come to seem true—beliefs. Are your beliefs and habits bringing you satisfaction? Contentment? Fulfillment?

Getting Back on Track

Here are some attitudes and habits to look out for and upgrade to get Desire working correctly again. Each one is a belief acquired along your journey, a subconscious adaptation that runs you like a computer program. These are, in fact, algorithms that you are as unaware of as the code in your apps. Carrying this analogy further, when you look into the code and find the glitch, you can reprogram so life runs smoothly. Change takes focus, learning, time and practice. Learn about these beliefs; some practices will follow.

Deserving

Every living thing wants to live and grow and needs lots of things to do so. If you are alive, you deserve to be here and to do your best to get what you need.

"I overachieve at work, take total responsibility for my household and take care of my parents. I felt the flu coming on and was actually in touch with my needs, my body's needs. For the first time, I rested in bed all weekend and didn't feel guilty and didn't get sick!" —Sarah

Feeling undeserving can be the belief driving people-pleasers and those who give and give to their detriment and even when returned with abuse. Here, shame and self-esteem are needed. A good practice is to learn to ask yourself, "What do I want?" before agreeing to anything new. At first, you may not go the next step to honoring your needs, but knowing them will lead to that next step.

Taking Responsibility

Your life is your responsibility. Your needs are yours. Others will help, but your needs never become someone else's job. Watch out for expectations and demands for what others should do for you. Blaming and complaining about what you don't have is a poor substitute for doing what you can to take care of yourself.

"I can't believe how I've put my needs in men's hands, waiting for them to take care of me and solve all my problems. I'm tired of feeling like a beggar! Actually, I am more capable than any man I've been with. I've realized that I am the one I have been waiting for; I am my own hero." —S.W.

Don't Let Past Needs or Future Fantasies Ruin Reality

Things you needed when you were 3, 6, 12, 18, or yesterday and did not get, leave a mark, a little hole that you want to fill. While many needs like love and security are with us throughout our years, many others change. And how to best fulfill needs must change as we grow or we get stuck in ineffective or injurious habits. You can get stuck pining for something you don't need now.

Gloria is 63 and came to me unhappy that she needed more excitement and badly wanted a man in her life. When I helped her see a clear image of marriage after all these years on her own, she realized how much she loved her freedom and independence. Her desires were leftover from her late teens and 20s and how her friends live. Letting those go, she realized all she needed now was to take those classes she had wanted and do some traveling.

The mind's ability to anticipate future needs is a great advantage in taking care of ourselves. Planning can make something ready when you get there: a hotel reservation so you have a place to stay, training for a job so you have a source of income, savings and insurance for a time you will need it. Imagination, dreams and fantasies are so powerful and real we can miss out on what we need here and now. How often is a relationship, a vacation, any planned event—including how we imagine our life to play out—ruined because it is not what we envisioned? Mindful awareness of desires can separate our real and present needs from all the noise of memory, external influence and imagination.

Self-Care is a Learned Skill

If you found yourself the caretaker of a rare and exotic animal, you would have to learn what it needs in order for it to be healthy and happy. You are that unique and beautiful creature and you are your caretaker: get good at your job. The care and feeding of your own precious, needy, worthy self is a skill. Pay attention to your ups and downs, physical, mental, emotional and spiritual health. Needs continuously change, so keep learning.

> *"I didn't realize I need to figure out what I need; I thought it was automatic." —Eliz. S.*

Substitutes That Don't Hit the Spot

When you feel lonely and eat, the food becomes a companion and eating feels a bit like love. Since it is neither, eating must continue to unsuccessfully satisfy. This underlies many addictions. Orgasm is not intimacy, being busy does not fulfill purpose, having many likes and followers is not a lasting sense of self-worth. It's like taking B vitamins when you need C: you are doing something but not the things that you need. Coming up is an exercise to feed the real need.

> *"My husband is always working; we never relate. I eat a lot of candy and run up the credit cards shopping, but I wish we were close like before." —D.K.*

> *"I'm a school junkie, always going for more degrees. My desire has always been to create art, but my parents' fears about making a living killed that dream. So, I keep learning instead." —E. S.*

Beware the Habit of Hunger

Our physical needs are ever-recurring; you eat your fill but say 'I'm starving" again in a few hours. This can create perpetual insecurity—"will it be there next time?" When needs are chronically in short supply, especially in our formative years, it is common to develop the habit to need, a pattern of seeking but rarely getting, even when there is plenty available. Uncovering the underlying beliefs, such as not deserving and practicing to get what you seek can resolve such patterns.

Recurring physical needs create the mistaken idea that non-physical needs are insatiable. "I've had a long and fulfilling career, but now that it is over, I feel so empty." Psychological needs need not be insatiable; they are thoughts based in beliefs and bound by memories. Look again at the earlier list of needs. You have had many separate moments experiencing many of them. Pick one and recall such feelings of satisfying that need, feeling appreciated, etc. Think of these moments as precious gems you are gathering in a basket as you go through life. Your basket can become ever more full of these riches you value. By the end of your life you feel wealthy and complete. But if these important experiences don't stay with you, as if your basket has no bottom so nothing sticks, you are forever seeking more. This way, you would likely die feeling empty and wanting. Let appreciation, connection, or a sense of value supply you with your own internally regenerating feelings of the same.

Learning to Receive

It is surprising to discover that you may badly want and your wishes may be available, but you never actually get it. Worse, you have it and don't realize; you still feel empty. You may need praise to feel good about yourself but can't accept a compliment. You may need love and live many years with a loyal partner and feel unloved. We'll practice this in the next meditation.

"I've complained forever that I have to do everything and my husband doesn't do anything for me. Seeing my need for kindness, for once I asked that he help out. Weird, but when he started bringing me tea at night, I felt really uncomfortable. But I'm getting to like it! Next goal, him making money and helping pay the bills." —S.M.

You Need to Speak Your Needs

Even those who love you can't guess what you need. They are busy trying to get theirs. But they may help if you ask.

"I'm always cranky. None of my needs are being met. I hate having to ask anybody for anything. I seem to believe that people should just know my needs. Like me! I am acutely aware of other peoples' needs and utterly unaware of my own. I married my exact opposite, someone who is very clear of their own needs, has not the least bit of trouble asserting himself but is completely unaware that I have needs. I've been trying to please other people by fulfilling their needs, in hopes they will reciprocate." —A.F.

Who's in Control Here?

This whole business of Desire is a bit messy; what are we to do with it? What is the goal here? Certainly, to be free of "too much or too little" dysfunction to start. Better yet, to be attentive and responsive to our needs, which will reduce much stress and upset. But what do you really need? How do you know what is best for you and to what end? How to control these desires? And will they bring happiness?

The challenge of Desire, as with all emotions, is that it takes control of us and when we lose control, things get messy. So then, control your emotions! How well is that working for humanity? The middle way is to work in partnership with emotion, with Desire, to align with its truth. There is fascinating brain research that shows activity occurs in the brain that initiates our desire to do or have something before we have the thought that we want it. The implication is that desires arise and we respond rather than have free will to choose; I don't choose what I desire, I only feel a desire and act accordingly. Is it our brain, our animal nature, God, or all three controlling us? It certainly seems to us that we are in control, but look at how poor humanity is at regulating our urges. In this light, how is emotional liberation possible?

The foundational premise of this work is that emotions contain wisdom. Contrary to our troubles with emotions, they are to be listened to, trusted and obeyed. Obeyed rather than controlled? Yes, by honestly, deeply listening to our feelings, unfiltered by our history and habits, we can trust what we find. We have to listen without thinking, to feel without filters.

The first exercise in this chapter was meant to check your sensory system for the ability to feel and get in touch with Desire. Following were several exercises in self-assessment, questions to help you understand aspects of how you relate to and use Desire. Now we will go back into direct experience of the emotion, listening to it through intellect and intuition. Here is the sequence of needs one student discovered in this meditation, along with the type of need:

> "I want to eat healthier..." (a need to do something)
> "...so I will be skinnier..." (a need to be something)
> "...so I will be a good singer and dancer..."

(doing and being needs)

"...for my dad to be proud of me..." (to receive something)

"...so I can feel good about myself and that he cares about me..." (to feel some things)

"...Maybe then Dad will quit drinking..." (an additional effect of doing)

"...and my mum and dad will have a happy marriage..." (to have happy parents)

"... so I have a family that stays together..." (to have something)

"...so I can feel safe and loved" (her deepest need and end game goal).

Our Desires are all directed toward experience, preferred, positive experiences. Her physical desires may not be available, but the paths to experience love and safety are unlimited. Discover your needs and follow them to the deeper experiences that bring ultimate fulfillment.

Feeding Your Deepest Needs:
The Essential Practice for Desire[1]

To prepare your ability to listen to Desire, we'll use the breathing technique from earlier in the chapter. Sit comfortably in a quiet place where you will not be disturbed. Set a timer for six minutes and close your eyes. Breathe in through puckered lips and exhale through your nose with a soft hmmm sound. Focus on your lips, which are so sensitive to feel the cool air. You use them for pleasures like kissing and tasting.

---

[1] Guided meditation available at www.emotional-liberation.com/resources

These sensations connect you to Desire. Listen to the intimate whisper of the wh-oooooo sound of your inhale and that universal sound of satisfaction as you exhale. Continue steadily, bringing your mind back to focusing on the sounds and sensations for six minutes or more until you feel calm and clear in your mind, peaceful and secure in your body. When memories and emotions arise, stay connected to breath and body, observing without the mind becoming busy. Ask your body these questions and let the answers come by way of feelings rather than thoughts.

Now recall any stress, upset, or argument that comes to mind, a recurring or one-time event. Just as clearly as you were observing your breath, see the scene in your memory. From the thought, a wave of emotion will arise. Ask the feeling what it needs right at that moment. Is it something that you want to have or to happen? Now look further. Why is that important? What will you get from that? Offer yourself anything and imagine it happening; what makes it better for you? Now go one layer deeper: if these things happen, how do you hope to feel—about the situation, about yourself, about life and the other person, all people? Again you can imagine having that feeling right now. Let those feelings flow all through every part of your body. Use your imagination to satisfy these needs.

Now examine this deepest kind of need, to feel certain qualities. You may get to those feelings through the objects and actions you desire, but the feelings are not limited to those conditions. There are many other ways—unlimited different ways. You just achieved the feelings, or can learn to, by merely thinking. Imagine some other real-world conditions to help you get to these same feelings. When you feel complete with your process, bring yourself back with a few deep breaths and slowly open your eyes. Record your experiences.

Here are some realizations about Desire that many have had.

Beyond immediate life-and-death needs, the end game of emotional reactions, problems and challenges are psychological needs like security, acceptance, confidence, self-worth and freedom (i.e., all of column three and much of column two on the Needs List in Chapter 5.)

Psychological needs are thoughts, so you can generate them internally, as you may have done in the meditation. You are your own most reliable source of your deepest needs, a store that never closes. That gives you control, power and freedom to create your own happiness.

While objects and actions are finite and may not be readily available to you, psychological needs are non-physical and unlimited, so they are always available and no one can keep them from you. You are not dependent on any one person, source, or strategy to obtain them. There are infinite paths to freedom and security. Diversify your needs sources; there is no reason to be held hostage by one person, no single situation can totally limit your ability to get what you need. Having identified your needs, now examine how you have been trying to meet them and how well it has or has not been working. Practice listing three or four new and different approaches to directly and more effectively fulfill yourself with each need.

In this way, I have overcome personal addictions to food, to work and to pleasing others. I moved from the unending pusuit of enjoyment, which resulted in feeling "not enough', to simple joy. You can too. Joy and Enjoy are sisters. Enjoy comes to you from a physical source and is temporary. Joy can be with you at any time, without a physical prompt. You can call her up anytime and she can stick around as long as you can receive her. We act as if the two are co-dependent, but Joy is an infinite quality always available regardless of our short-term satisfactions. She travels with Contentment and they are both willing to move in with you.

Chapter 6

Restore Safety:
Use Fear to Find Peace

*"...let me assert my firm belief that the only thing we have to
fear is fear itself—nameless, unreasoning, unjustified terror
which paralyzes needed efforts to convert retreat into
advance." Franklin D. Roosevelt's First Inaugural Address*
(1933)

You may not personally be facing war or famine, but first
world, middle-class fears are just as real and debilitating. As
with trauma, we need not compare or defend our experience;
we all want to feel at peace. Based on day-to-day quality of life,
common threats we face and average lifespan, this is the safest
time to be a human on planet Earth. Yet anxiety, general stress
levels and related depression are epidemic. "Deaths of
Despair" and lifestyle-related disease show that the most
significant thing we have to fear is ourselves. There is much
out there that can harm you as well. That is why we are born
with a sensitive radar defense system to detect and avoid
harm; it is our Fear. Its purpose is to bring us to safety. Why
has it become a problem instead of serving to solve our
problems?

Paradoxically, though we are feeling so much fear, we
have become insensitive to it. Our great intellects over-think
and override the instincts that have served survival for
millions of years. We are too busy outrunning our fears to stop
and listen to the messages that seek to save us. It is clear to me
why my students gain quick and profound results from

working mindfully with their emotions. They take the time and effort to pay attention to, get to know and work with their emotions. Not repress, hide from, deny, overrule, become numb to the discomfort of their feelings, but to feel and face them. In the case of Fear, the best way to get out of Fear is to go through it. Fear is your friend! It is an accurate threat detector for all that would disturb your well-being.

While Desire is the positive message of what you *do* want, its complementary opposite is Fear, which shows you what you *don't* want. Imagine using their partnership to avoid the pain of lack and wanting. Let's now dive into the darkness of Fear to find the light of Peace. Our process will be to first change our thinking about Fear from foe to friend: it is not a problem; it solves problems. This thinking will help your willingness to dip in and feel your Fear, spend time and develop a working relationship as you would with any powerful partner. In time, as you become more comfortable with it, you quiet the confusion Fear creates in your head. Without that noise, instinct becomes intuition. You learn from the past instead of being stuck in it, you relax about the future knowing you can trust Fear to warn ahead of time and give you the energy to stay out of harm's way.

The Purpose of All Fears

An internet search will give you many systems that name and categorize fears. The *Diagnostic and Statistical Manual of Mental Disorders* (*DSM–5*) lists five categories of specific phobias within which there are thousands of specific things we fear. Each one has or can be given a scientific name. Why do we have so much fear? I invite you to understand Fear through personal research, using your direct experience and a simple model:

The purpose of Fear is safety.
Fear senses danger and seeks safety.

Fear gathers information and takes action to avoid harm. In an immediate crisis, Fear works automatically, quickly and, most often, reliably as an automatic reflex. But in most of our non-emergency situations, when we have time to think about what to do, our thinking complicates and even interferes: we fail to recognize or act on the threat or to create the safety that relieves our Fear. Knowing its purpose makes all the difference: when you feel Fear, identify the threat and what will bring you to safety. This is a simple core practice we will come back to. This first step is simply to begin thinking of Fear as an ally, not an enemy. All those disturbing thoughts and feelings are like those annoyingly loud fire alarms, designed to get your attention in a hurry—they are trying to help save you.

Get Clear About Your Fear

Next, you need material to work with, so take a clear look at your relationship with Fear. Here's a story to get you started.

> "There are no immediate major threats in my life, yet I feel tense, anxious and uneasy most all the time. I worry about my kids, am I a good mother, do we have enough money, lots of things. My mind is always on the go. I have to-do lists I look at often but don't get much done and then feel I'm not achieving. Maybe it started in my 20s when I started working full time at a daunting new job. After the breakup of a long relationship, I didn't feel safe on my own and lost a lot of weight. There was a lot of

tragedy in my parents' early life; when I grew up and to this day, my family lives in fear quite a bit about getting sick, financial security and personal safety. I just never felt safe, though all that happened to me was that my family was always critical or ridiculing of my sensitive nature." —Mina

Notice the various parts of her story, which tells us about her relationship with Fear. You have yours, too. Every relationship has many aspects which together create the whole picture. Below are examples shared with me by fully functional, successful people like those you see and work with every day. They are categorized to show the many elements of a Fear story. Use the list to identify your fears and know that you are normal and not alone in having them.

Forms and Signs of Fear: worry, doubt, overwhelm, out of control, confusion, insecurity, lack of confidence, panic, anxiety, terror

Things That Trigger My Fears: workload, deadlines and mistakes at work; bills and debt, when my partner is mad at me, memories of when I was abused, walking alone at night

What Happens in My Body: "butterflies" in my stomach, tightness in my jaw, neck and belly, lack of appetite and indigestion, a nervous pressure in my chest and my heart is racing

What Goes Through My Head: Will it happen? What if...? What do they think? Do they like me? Will I get the job? Can I keep the job? Will he leave me? Do I have enough money? What will happen when I get old?

What I Do: I get hyper. I can't stop eating. I don't eat much and don't enjoy food. I get confused and can't make decisions. I live in a state of overwhelm. I shut down and can't do anything. I can't speak up when I don't like what's happening. I reacted instinctively and swerved out of the way. I leave any confrontative conversation or relationship. I'm afraid to spend money, so things like my unrepaired car become dangerous. Something goes wrong, but I don't do anything, so it gets worse. I just can't get the nerve to ask her to go out with me.

History and Past Fears: My dad would continuously tell us as kids that we needed to pack our bags because we did not have enough for rent and we were going to be homeless. He seemed to enjoy this. But by the second week of the month, the money would come through and he would say, "See, I can always scrape enough up." I had severe pain in my stomach for weeks and thought it was cancer. My ex-husband would blow up at me at any time. My company was bought and down-sized. For a year, we all expected to be fired. I got separated from my nursery school class on a field trip and wandered scared and alone for hours. I'll never forget looking out the window at my father leaving us on our own; he never came back.

Present Fears: Look out for that car! The microwave is sparking and smoking! The pain in my side is unbearable—what is happening to me?

Future Fears: I have a new job and worry whether I can do it and what will they think of me. (Notice that the situation is in the present, but the fear is of the future.)

Existential and Macro Fears: Vaccinations are harmful. They are tracking all our data. Climate change makes me not want to have children. I'm not afraid of death, but pain and incapacity terrify me. The government is making those chemtrails to poison us. Watching my father's Alzheimer's progress freaks me out about getting older. Will people ever stop fighting and hurting each other?

Your Fear Sources and Solutions

This exercise starts with getting your body moving to better connect with feelings. First, identify something from your life in every category above. It may be uncomfortable or unpleasant, easier not to look at yourself, but every cure starts with knowing the signs and symptoms. With that information, we can get to the causes and remedies.

When you know why Fear arises and what to do about it, the threat and the way to safety—and you do it—you feel better and move on in relative peace. The epidemic of chronic anxiety and stress shows the dire need to improve this skill. Applying the SOS Method described in Chapter 5 with an understanding of Fear's purpose, we get the following self-inquiry. You can simply think about these questions, but better to ask and answer them mindfully. Or try it both ways.

First, choose a fear to work with. Find a quiet space and time to practice. Run in place for five minutes. Imagine you are running for your life away from death itself. Feel the fear and push to get exhausted. If running is a problem, lie on a padded surface and shake your body. Feel nervous and scared, freak out, twitching and shaking every muscle and nerve for the full five minutes. Then sit or lie comfortably, close your eyes and feel your breath, heartbeat and any other internal sensations you notice. Let your mind become still along with your body; stay focused on the senses rather than having wandering thoughts. When you feel reasonably calm and clear, recall the situation you want to address vividly in your mind. Let feelings arise in your body, focus with curiosity on the sensations and the energy of Fear. Let it all happen. Observe without judgment or resistance. Imagine these feelings to be your friend Fear, communicating with you. When you ask these questions, let your body respond rather than your mind.[2]

/ /

---

[2] Guided meditation available at www.emotional-liberation.com/resources

1. What am I feeling? Allow and identify the feelings and any other emotions that may join in. Focus now only on the Fear. When you are ready, ask:

2. Why am I feeling this? Relax; don't try hard. Let answers come from your body and the feelings themselves. It's usually apparent at the surface what is bothering you, but go deeper. Why is this a threat? How will it hurt me? Get to the actual source. Thoughts will come but stay with the body as much as you can.

3. What do I need to be safe? How do I avoid the danger or deal with it? What will make this okay so I feel better, more secure and relaxed? Imagine knowing or doing anything you wish, no matter how outrageous or practical.

4. Take whatever you find and now bring in the mind to strategize how you can use this information and ideas to bring yourself to safety and resolve the fears.

Put Together Your Fear Story

When you finish the session, write about what you found and commit yourself to next steps. A situation might not be resolved simply and all at once, but clarity and action move you in the direction of peace. Make it a work in progress and keep working with Fear. Over time you will eliminate constant threats you may be tolerating in the present, clear up old fears from the past and begin to trust Fear to serve you well in the future anytime it is needed. This is a description of trusting yourself and the Universe so you can deeply relax.

Dysfunctional Fear

How does this defensive emotion that evolved over millions of years—and without which no animal species would have survived—go wrong? Sh*t happens! So, even fully functional Fear can't always save us from harm. But if we work well with Fear, we can avoid all but unavoidable suffering. As with all protective emotions, there two opposite ways we misuse Fear: too much and too little.

When Fear takes over and controls us in non-reflexive situations, irrational Fear may not make the right decision. I want my hand to automatically protect me from a fall without thinking, but when I do harm to a loved one I suspect of infidelity because I haven't heard from them, Fear is controlling me and makes things worse.

The other end of the misuse spectrum is numbness, repression and denial of Fear. Your PFC-originated thoughts and beliefs override your limbic system-originated instinct that something doesn't feel right.

"I was just 4 when my "creep meter" told me that my parents' weird friend was trouble. They told me I was silly and that he was a good guy. He wasn't! But I kept ignoring those feelings right through college and a lot of bad relationships."

She was told to believe her parents instead of her feelings, creating a habit of overriding her protective gut reactions with their beliefs.

The middle way that works is to utilize intellect and emotion together. In the SOS Method for Fear above, the physical movement is to help you feel energized and willing to feel strong emotions and assist PFC activation for the following mindfulness. Voluntarily calling up the memory of harm activates emotion from the limbic system. When the two remain active without one overriding the other, you don't deny the feeling or overact, but can intelligently see what you need to know or do. Fear functions well. Paradoxically, fearful experiences can disrupt your ability to use Fear; being terribly or chronically unsafe can leave us feeling permanently insecure. In trauma, we can lose our ability to use Fear to avoid danger.

Fear and Trauma

Feeling trapped and powerless in a crisis, being unable to do anything about being harmed, significantly increases trauma. When newborn and in the early years we are most vulnerable and most sensitive. Early childhood dangers are felt intensely at a time we are least able to do what Fear requires for relief: do something to get safe.

Fear warns automatically, but your response is required. You could do nothing back then, danger remained, so Fear also continued, perhaps along with the belief that there is nothing you can ever do. That belief condemns you to always be in danger; Fear must remain ever-present. That is called hypervigilance and chronic anxiety. Consciously processing your fears can resolve them.

See here how Jasmine's early abuse and living in an unsafe home had long-term effects and that with help and personal efforts, she found that as an adult she can create her own security.

> " I have lived most of my life in a perpetual state
> of fear. I grew up in a very violent house. Mom

was beaten daily and we kids were spanked with a paddle until I was 8; verbal and emotional abuse until I left home. I've had insomnia since 3 and mastered looking cool while actually terrified and hyper-alert always.

Before I began dealing with my fear, I held the same anxiety and terror I felt as a young child. I didn't understand my experiences or have words for my feelings, I just lived with the physical tension and memories. Drastic improvement in 3 years now from using the SOS Method and some bodywork techniques— I move in my body and through life more freely. I discovered I have anger and also loneliness, a fear of being left alone.

I had an argument today with my boyfriend. I was really upset and went away to cry. I sat crying and mentally pleading for him to come say or do something to make me feel better. Then I remembered to ask myself what I needed to feel better and I had this internal dialogue— 'He's not coming, stop expecting him to. No one is coming, not to see your pain, to make you feel better or to save you. No one ever has come or helped much. Anytime you were saved, you did it yourself. You are the only one who can make you feel better. How awesome is that!? Who is better fit for the job and who knows you better than you know yourself and who is ALWAYS with you and can see and feel when you need them? You've had this best friend WITHIN you and you haven't even realized it. You get to take care of yourself the way you've wanted your parents, partners and friends to do. Start right now, taking responsibility and stop blaming them!'

I got up, I washed my face, put my hand on my heart, breathed deeply and felt so much better; liberated, cared for, loved. I've gone through life with this belief (I uncovered it earlier with the triggers worksheet) that no one cares about me. My fear of loneliness came from not caring enough about myself. So grateful to have found this." —Jasmine

Jasmine did a lot of work that culminated in this realization. But this is more than an epiphany: her life changed forever. People had told her and she'd read self-help books saying these same beautiful things. I'm sure you have used affirmations and positive thinking as well. But when you hear your truth from the inside, it is real, it is you and there is no doubt. This is why self-therapy is so effective. Never again will she tolerate abuse or neglect, withdraw or not defend herself; never again will she be treated that way. Those effects of her early trauma are resolved and healed. Here is our measure of trauma healing as related to Fear:

"When I can make myself safe now, in situations in which I was unsafe before, I have recovered my ability to be safe and am healed."

Fear seeks safety and security, which are fierce biological needs. When you adequately fulfill your need for protection, Fear's purpose is accomplished and it steps down; you can relax and enjoy life. Your need for safety and your fear of harm are partners. Working with both will significantly increase your peace and contentment.

The Marriage of Fear and Desire

Fear and Desire are a polarity; they define and complete each other. The negatives in Fear and the positives in Desire form a complete picture of your well-being. All fears are in response to needs and needs are the domain of Desire. This brings us back to Needs as the source of triggers and traumas. When you don't get what you need, the absence of that thing now 'endangers' your well-being compared to your having obtained it. Let's say you live with a partner after living on your own for years. After a breakup, you are anxious about being on your own and worry you might never again find such a love.

Fear is, therefore, a negative indicator of your positive desire. If trauma is caused by a violated need, then Fear will be right there with you as the most urgent emotion for the job. In the traumatic experience, it unsuccessfully seeks information and action to escape. Unable to do its job, Fear goes into a hair-trigger hyper-alert mode, trying to avoid what the mind remembers you could not prevent before. Your adapting brain, eager to learn a lesson from the crisis that will evade that same danger in the future, locks onto those spontaneous thoughts, feelings and responses—however ineffective—and they are recycled later when you actually have a much higher capacity and options.

> *"If I talked back to my father when he yelled at me, I got smacked. To this day, when my boss takes a firm tone, or my partner is unhappy with me, I can't say a word and just want to run."*

When frightened again, the mind calls on the response it used as a child. All the growth and learning of many years is unavailable when our old reaction is activated by a similar trigger. We shut down or lash out as before and safety remains out of reach. Mindful use of Fear, practiced at first by reviewing or previewing a triggering situation, will bring to mind and make available more age-appropriate and effective responses, which can eventually be available in real time. Mindful work with Desire is an equally critical path to reclaiming peace after trauma.

When love, safety and other crucial needs are cut off, it is common to become stuck focusing on the fear of what you *don't* want. How can you solve the problem of not having something? Only by identifying what you *do* want and need. The immediate terror of a near collision doesn't want you hurt or killed; the need is safety. The fear of a serious medical diagnosis doesn't want you to be sick; the need is survival, vitality and enjoyment rather than pain. The fearful memories of a past trauma don't want it to happen to you again; the need is security. Anxiety about finances is a desire for security, autonomy, freedom and ease. Fear of losing a relationship may be a desire for sex, intimacy, connection and support. The fear of public speaking or social shaming doesn't want you to be rejected; the desire is for acceptance and self-esteem. Worries over species extinction may be a desire for the beauty nature brings.

The mind gets stuck like one of those irritating car alarms when no one checks for a break-in, telling you over and over what you don't want. It's got no game. Make the fear tell you precisely what it doesn't want, then go under that to identify what you *do* want. Like throwing a ball for an enthusiastic dog to fetch, this gives the mind a specific task to pursue for you. Your mind is built to go after things, so shifting your focus from Fear to your underlying desires is a way to get unstuck from a persistent unresolved fear.

Your work in the Desire chapter was to identify your wants and deepest needs. Fulfilling them will reduce both immediate fears and the insecurity of being unable to do so as they come. Make a list of your past, present and future fears, worries, concerns and doubts. One at a time, close your eyes and focus on that thought until feelings come along with it. Simply ask your body, your heart, what does that fear show you that you want. With any answers you get, imagine them happening. Your better feelings, relief of fear is an accurate confirmation. If you don't think it is possible, don't give up on that solution, but also ask for something smaller and seemingly quite possible that moves you toward better feelings of ease.

Is the puzzle of why you do and feel things you don't like becoming clearer? Are you closer to solving it? Here is a woman's story that ties together trauma, fears and needs—proof that trauma creates beliefs and patterns that can be replaced. To break down how Fear broke down and left her unsafe, I have separated it into pieces with titles and commentary to show the role of each part of her story.

Ashley's Story of Recovering Safety

What Stuck Looks Like:

> *"I don't think of myself as a fearful person, but I realize I live with very little security. I look like I'm fine, but we three live in a cramped storage room and could be evicted anytime. My husband rarely works and I quit three promising careers, thinking I wouldn't be able to succeed—and I haven't. I do worry about health, but never about money. This week I had*

my decayed tooth extracted and thought, 'How did I let my life get so bad, how did I get so bad at looking after myself?'"

(Fear seeks safety. She doesn't feel it anymore and it isn't bringing her security. She lives with the cumulative effects of this.)

How She Got There:

> "My stepdad was not a safe person to be around; he had an explosive temper when disciplining my brother and me when we were young. As a teenager, he picked fights and got physically violent. My mum always defended him, not me. She modeled ignoring one's own safety by staying in that abusive relationship. Any care and kindness she could spare went to my seriously ill brother."

Danger was frequent and became normalized. There were no environmental cues that safety was possible; instead, her role model lived in danger.

Coping Strategy:

> " I found that if I disregarded my own needs for comfort, she was happier with me because I was one less thing to deal with."

To have no needs, including safety, was rewarded with her mother's approval, or at least less rejection.

Belief:

> *"My health didn't seem important to her. I accepted that my needs, my safety were not to be expected, that I was not worth protecting."*

She felt unworthy of love and protection and expected to live without them.

Resulting Behaviors:

> *"So, I never went to my parents for help with several big experiences when I was in danger. I can see why I put myself in really unsafe situations and did risky behaviors in my early twenties, on to several terrible relationships that really damaged me emotionally. My husband now is comparatively safe; it's neglect instead."*

Her belief expects, creates and allows abuse and neglect.

Realization: Fears Work to Help Fulfill Needs

> *"I can see now why I've let my life get really messy. I just haven't listened to my fears because, as I didn't consider my safety to be important, I didn't even know being safe was an option. It's mostly relationships that trigger my fears. I don't feel safe with people, so I am friendly but avoid more extended contact. I've had the volume on my fear turned down, so I've just had to avoid people. My radar can't tell who is safe and who isn't, so now I just keep most people out and work hard instead.*

Relationships are a source of pleasure but not for me. I wonder if I'm having a relationship with sugar instead of humans. Feeling safe is one of the needs I've been ignoring, the very need fear is supposed to handle. No wonder I've been relentlessly suppressing my fear; by disregarding my need to be safe, I ignored fear and that allowed all the bad situations to build up."

She sees that she lacks security with people and she needs Fear to help her find safety within relationships. Her need for connection isn't satisfied without that security; she uses food to fill the void, which is not the same and leaves her wanting.

Fear Speaks to Create Safety:

"Fear has been telling me to speak up. It introduced me to my anger, lost long ago. I started setting boundaries and getting back to work that I ran from. I'm in a beautiful living space now and making some money. I am actually really good at taking care of myself."

After years of poor self-care, the result of early trauma, Ashley paid attention to her emotions, which helped guide her into action. Fear identified the problem, Anger brought protection so she could take care of herself and satisfy desires.

From Fear to Trust

By now, it should be clear that our goal is not to be rid of Fear or any other emotion that feels uncomfortable. They are hardwired into our nervous system and evolved to serve us.

Fear arises when something you need is under threat and Fear leaves when you do what you can to take care of yourself. This is an important distinction: do what you can to take care of yourself and make the best of things. All things come and go; we cannot stop the natural cycle of life. We cannot avoid the threats that are inherent to existence—existential threats. The fact that we can never be safe from all harm does not mean we can never be at peace. Fear does not require it.

When you listen to Fear and find its wisdom, realizing what you need to know or do will bring immediate relief to anxious feelings. For lasting relief, you must put into practice anything you recognize and that takes two forms. Doing what you can to further your well-being takes physical action to prevent or get out of avoidable trouble: aligning income and expenses for financial security, attending to the many aspects of maintaining health, handling or eliminating toxic relationships. But some things are beyond your control: the actions of people you read about in the news, destructive human behavior in general, the power of nature we call natural disasters when living things are harmed, disease and death, that the sun itself will die one day. These existential fears are handled not by action but by information, understanding, by thinking about them in a way that changes our relationship to the threat and brings peace of mind.

Everybody dies, but some approach death with dread, others with acceptance and some embrace it gladly to be "going home." Accepting and making the best of what you cannot change are thoughts that create a kind of security. It is possible to live in unsafe situations—this world will always have conflict and natural disasters—yet live with peace of mind. To change what you can and accept what you can't change is wisdom that is required if you want to live in this world with serenity. *"God, grant me the serenity to accept the things I cannot change, courage to change the things I can and wisdom to know the difference"* has become a useful motto in recovery programs globally. How to live it? To truly accept one's fragile place in creation requires Trust. We usually feel safe and happy when everything goes the way we want it to. When, in the darkest times, we trust that this, too, is just how it is, we can be at peace. It is possible to be in pain but not suffer additionally from the fear of it. This trust and acceptance come only with sincere effort to realize them. Working deeply, meditatively and honestly with Fear can achieve this. Don't stay stuck with what it tells you that you don't want; let it shine a light on what you do want and need to be at peace.

Chapter 7

Reclaim Power:
Use Anger to Take Care of Yourself

We've all been hurt. From social rejection and broken dreams to crippling injuries, life's a school of hard knocks. Wherever there is harm, Anger arises. It is the emotion that brings us the power to protect and to "go get." It is the energy that fuels strong reactions to things we don't like or want. It is feared because of widespread misuse, but Anger's heat can better be used to be protective and productive. Its higher purpose is to guard and build rather than attack and destroy. Despite our collective legacy of generations of abuse, you can find your power and use it to great benefit. In this chapter, I will help you reclaim empowering uses of Anger to take control of the inner and outer challenges. We see how Anger is misused, generationally inherited and how to exit this cycle of abuse personally.

With the help of Desire and Fear, you will always know what you want and what you don't want. Then you will need the power to go get it. You may still carry patterns that make it challenging to acquire your desires. The power to speak up and obtain what you need, which is often lost in trauma, is recovered by working with Anger. It is common to relate Fear to fight, flight, or freeze. But Fear's job is to sound the alarm like the guard in the watchtower. The action of responding to handle the situation is the job of Anger, the energy behind the warriors who answer the alarm cry to defend the queen. We know Anger for its fight, but flight is sometimes the best defense. To freeze—in the case of an opossum and an abused child—may sometimes be the right reaction. But freezing can also be the inability to access Anger to protect yourself. We start Anger-work with this renewed concept: protection is what Anger is all about.

Don't judge Anger as good or bad but rather, like fire and nuclear energy, by how it is used and the effects it has. With too little, you are overpowered by circumstances and taken advantage of by others. With too much you are the bull in a china shop, clumsily using brute force where skill and carefulness work better. After all the harm we have felt, seen and done ourselves, it takes time and direct experience to accept Anger and put it to good use. Once you realize Anger's protective potential and contrast that with its many misuses, you must activate it where dormant and safely discharge its excess, retraining that inner beast to be your loyal bodyguard under attack and work to handle learnable life skills no matter how dysfunctional your past. We begin with a true story typical of how Anger's dysfunctions are learned.

Daia's History with Anger

> "My father psychologically abused my mother for years, then left her for his mistress when I was young. It was total abandonment, leaving my mum with full responsibility for their four young children. Next came my stepfather who was mean to me and abusive to my mother. When I would get mad at him about it as a teenager, he would rage and hurt me. I learned to keep quiet and out of the way, but took all my frustrations out on my submissive mother. When this made things worse, all my fight went quiet. I became wildly self-destructive and then fell into depression. I came out of that

depression and put a lot of energy into my final year at high school, knowing that if I did well at school, the University was my ticket out of the situation. Ever since, when I don't like what is happening, I mostly say nothing but have occasional angry outbursts. In recent years, my stress levels have increased and my angry outbursts have become more frequent and intense. I've started to feel like my anger bank is getting really full and I can no longer contain it. I'm turning back again from a repressor into an expresser." —Daia

In this story, everyone is failing to use their power to get what they need. The energy is either too much, too little, or misdirected. The father wants love but doesn't know how to get it, hurts people and then tries again with others. The mother wants safety but finds only harm in her partner, leaves the toxic relationship, has to do everything herself, then finds more pain in the next partner. Daia finds little love or safety as a child, makes efforts to take care of herself first by expressing Anger, finds that makes life worse, then returns to passivity as protection, finally applying her energies to achievement to take care of herself. But the confusing misuses of Anger continue in her career and roles as a wife and mother. Think through and write out your lifetime experiences with Anger. Tracking your history will help you understand when it is too much, too little, or just right. Her story continues with misuses of Anger and how it affects her today.

Misused Expressions of Anger

"My mum is an anger suppressor. She doesn't think she is mad but withdraws love, continually complains and criticizes everyone

and is passive-aggressive—allowing bad things to happen which she could have prevented. My father and stepfather are expressers, big time. They yell, bully, taunt, demean, use physical force, economic control and manipulation and God knows what in the bedroom. My older brother is also a suppressor. My younger brother an expresser, my older sister seems to exist in a constant state of irritation, not suppressing but not expressing either in a messy mix of complaining, bitching, competing, jealousy, blaming, withdrawing. We're a pretty angry family come to think of it.

"I realized I am mad at myself for allowing things to happen, not defending myself, not speaking up. But I also feel guilty when I get angry and show it. The ability to use my voice was completely squashed. Trying to defend myself led to more significant harm. It is suppressed to the point that I feel unable to speak up for myself, either for protection or creativity in my work. I feel fearful about speaking up except with people that I'm very close to; I can totally go off on them. I find it difficult to make decisions, plagued by what is the 'right' choice. In my career, I am bullied by peers and quit, giving up on the work I want to do. I stood by and said nothing when my husband left his job in fear and hurt us financially. Instead, I took the financial burden on myself. I allow my son to misbehave, saying nothing until I lash out, neither of which change anything." —Daia

How do you use power in your life? Where is it underused, leaving you vulnerable and mistreated (too little)? When do you attack, harming others? Neither gets you what you want. And when is your power just right, protective with no harm to others and productive in taking care of yourself?

The Politics of Power and Empowerment

The results of skillfully working with Anger is refined, effective personal empowerment. You can help heal the effects of our violent human past at least in your own life by getting right your use of power. We are in a time of change where abuse is visible and condemned if not yet stopped. Long-oppressed classes of people are fighting for, if not yet always achieving, justice. Technology gives abusers and defenders greater reach. The individual can do greater good and harm. Power is democratizing. Old methods of control by force, inheritance, systems of oppression are being recognized and challenged. One of the most critical changes is women reclaiming their rightful power and the recognition of feminine forms of power. I expect the majority of you reading this book are reclaiming power; abusers take longer to recognize their way is not working. But "Power never gives up power willingly" (Howard Zinn), so you have some work to do. To further recognize and feel comfortable with your power, you need ways to safely release suppressed Anger that has accumulated from years of frustrations and harm. As you read these anonymous stories from others who have done this work, recognize your frustrating situations.

> *"I am afraid of Anger in myself and others. I feel mean and guilty when showing or even feeling it."*

"My ex-husband would accuse me of being angry and shame me for it. The message I got was it's a bad thing, especially for women. He could be mean, but if I spoke up, I was a bitch. He always won that way."

"I was raped. I recently realized that I constantly look for a fight to win and end up in situations that hurt me because being angry feels strong, which is better than that helpless feeling. I don't want to live in a constant state of Anger anymore."

"I am a woman in a male-dominated industry. I have to be powerful to compete. But feeling powerful feels mean; after making and winning my case, I later feel bad. I hold back my full talent and intelligence rather than risk disapproval or those shameful feelings."

"My father was always powerful and successful. He was critical of me, always wanting more and better but never affirming or pleased with me. So I tried harder and have succeeded well in my career. In spite of my success, I never feel powerful or successful. And where love and intimacy are involved, I lose my voice, feel powerless, unloved and am treated poorly, just as my father treated me."

"I feel so mad and ashamed of myself that I allowed and couldn't stop the abuse I received back then. Now, when I say, "STOP," I feel vulnerable and sad, that I am wrong even to say it."

Blowing Off Steam

When a person reacts angrily, or "blows up" more intensely than the situation warrants, they are acting out in part from their past unresolved hurts. People, like volcanoes, erupt when accumulated pressure overcomes whatever has blocked their Anger. Anger always transforms—for better or worse. When a pressure-cooker has a blocked relief valve, it blows up. Since most people have an unhealthy relationship with Anger, it grows. Once you resolve wounds from the past, little things won't upset you and you can better handle stress.

Here are some techniques to safely feel, express and release Anger that has been accumulating in you. Try one or all. First set a clear intention that you will harmlessly release Anger so you can move on, that you will no longer allow nor perpetuate harm.

/ /

Sit on the floor or in a chair. Close your eyes. Take a deep breath and hold it as you punch the air with tight fists, alternately straightening the arms completely. Punch fast and furiously until you need to exhale, then pause the punching to exhale, take another breath and continue. Get mad and imagine anyone and anything out there you are mad about. Go hard for three to five minutes. Then lie down on your back and laugh out loud (you might begin to cry), but not more than three minutes. Lie still, rest and be peaceful. Release heat, tension and Anger from your body like radiation leaving you. Give yourself the time to fall asleep if you can. Finally, rise lighter and refreshed. Drink some cool water and take it easy for a while. Make a few notes about your experience on the Anger pages you began earlier. You need to know you have strength and fierce fighting energy in you, that it can be controlled and safely expressed rather than feared and repressed.

/ /

"I found letting it out in a good tantrum is better than stewing on the issue all day."
—Allen

Try this exercise to identify and discharge your mental storage of Anger. Go to a place of privacy in your home or in the woods where no one can see or hear you. Set your intention to release Anger harmlessly so you can move on; mad thoughts about those who have harmed you can empower you and will not hurt them. Sit with eyes closed, or stand and walk as you begin consciously complaining about anything and everything in the world that is wrong with people, unfair in life, evil in the world. If you can let loose more fully inside your head, think these angry thoughts. If you want to verbalize, let it out of your mouth. Build the steam for no less than three minutes, no more than five. Part of your mind will take note of what you are saying; you may discover in this stream of consciousness what it is you are mad about, what you want and need to deal with and what you need to say (later and more calmly). Be sure to include telling people what they need to know or do. Record what you learn.

When Daia Let It Out

"I'm seen as a sweet, quiet woman, so it was hard to get started. I did a lot more complaining than I thought I would be able to. When I got started on my abusive, abandoning father and his mistress-to-become-step-mother, I was astonished at how much Anger roared out like, who is this person? Seems weird that I've never actually felt angry about

161

this (or realized it?). But oh my gosh! I had something to say about this during my 'sacred tantrum!' Also makes me angry that my mum is still mad about it after 35 years; neither of us is over it. I repressed, she expresses, but neither of us knows what to do with our Anger.

After I had exhausted this, I got onto the subject of white people!! Who would have thought that I had so much Anger towards white folk? I'm as white as anyone I know, but apparently, I think we're a bunch of f'ing a-holes." —Daia

Protective and Productive—Utilizing Anger's Energy

"I can feel my Anger. Now, how do I handle it?" —Sarah

"There's so much that I need to handle. Making some more money; getting my career back on track; taking care of me and my family's health; improving my living situation; bringing more enjoyment into my life. I really need to stand up for myself and stop letting those other a-holes at work psych me out of doing what I am good at." —Daia

Once you can accept and recognize Anger and discharge it to a workable level, now learn to work *with* it. The evolutionary purpose of Anger is to "Protect and Go Get". When you are hurt, it seeks to stop the harm and prevent it from going forward—Anger is for protection. Anything you can't do, handle, arrange, take care of for your benefit harms you as compared to if you could get it done—Anger is for

Production, which also protects you from the harm of not having. You can take the reins of this wild emotional beast and have it plow your fields.

Whenever You Find Yourself Angry: Stop, Feel and Recover

First, know when you are feeling it. Learn to recognize Anger—perhaps later at first and eventually as it is occurring—in any of its forms or degrees: feeling bothered, annoyance, irritation, frustration, resentment, fury and rage; and the expressions of blaming, complaining, aggression, attacking, chronically criticizing, using sarcasm, sabotaging, withholding and other creative masking expressions. You are not an angry person nor a bad person. Instead, something has harmed you that you need to take care of. Once you are protected and things are reasonably handled, you will not feel angry—until Anger is required again. When you are mad, don't act yet! That will be an impulsive reaction in which the Anger energy is working on its own without your conscious guidance. If at all possible, get away from the triggering stimulus—the person that just pissed you off or the precious project you just ruined—until you can once again think clearly. As discussed previously, you need to engage the pre-frontal cortex—your intellect—to guide the emotion to its purpose.

Recovery Tips

- Stop everything. Count as you breathe ten long, deep and full breaths. Go longer as needed until you feel your body and mind deescalating.
- Get outside and walk in open spaces, fast at first then naturally slow down as you become calmer. Don't think about the issue at all until you feel

settled.

- Drink water. At least eight ounces right away. Hydration helps the nervous system.
- Cold water! Splash your face, full cold shower, jump in a pool.
- Talk yourself down as you would to encourage a friend: "It's going to be okay. I'm all right. I'll figure this out and deal with it. The earth will not end. This is not okay and I will make it right!"

Try any or all of these, or find your most effective Anger management tools.

///

Listen to Anger and Use it Well

Once you are "in your right mind," meditatively ask yourself some questions that will reveal Anger's purpose. Close your eyes. The calmer and more neutral you are while still in touch with your Anger, the clearer and more accurate the answers will be. Remember to listen for answers not from your "thinking mind" but from a deeper place; feel for the answers in your body.

"Why am I mad, really? Why does this upset me? What harm has happened/is happening to me? What is hurt: my body, my security, my feelings, my values, my future, my social standing, my self-respect, my heart, others that I care about, my control to have things my way?" You can ask anything. Explore with questions and listen for answers rather than "trying to solve it."

Once the real source of your Anger is clear, ask for solutions.

"Anger, what do you want? What do I need to know or do to take care of myself, to handle this situation?"

Continue to ask for clarity; ask to see how until you are satisfied. You may not like it or think you can do what you are shown—trusting your inner voice takes time. For now, remember and record what you discover. Write down anything you learn whether you understand it or not. In addition to resolving a situation, you are learning how to listen to your own internal guidance. Do this self-inquiry process not just during an upset, but afterward, when it is easier to calmly review it "from a distance." With practice, you will know what to do quickly and trust your actions.

Review old issues and memories of past wounds. Preview anticipated confrontations from a neutral state and ask your Anger how to navigate it. You will find your own answers. The next step is to act on them, which may take time and courage. But until things are handled, your reliable Anger bodyguard will resurface and let you know you are not yet protecting yourself.

Maria's Process

> *"Here's what I found when I talked with my Anger.*
>
> *What I feel—Angry with my sister. She dominates, takes advantage, criticizes and demeans me.*
>
> *Why I feel it—I was the younger sister, she would bully me and was Mom's favorite. To this day, they are close and take sides against me and take advantage of my easy-going generosity.*

What I need to do—I want to scream/kick/hit; I never did that as a child. I need to speak up to her, fight for myself, reclaim my power and protect myself now that I realize I have the strength. Write a letter to them. Love and forgive myself at that age for not fighting back; write a letter to myself about it. Love myself, believe in myself.

Actions to take—I've screamed—will do more! Have written a letter in my journal, need to write more. Will continue to practice self-love. Speak up from now on when I feel it's not right. Stay in my power; use it to protect my peace."
—Maria

Positive Power

Proper use of Anger means taking action that is right for the situation and does not expend energy without a worthwhile result. Harm and destruction are the all-too-familiar dark sides of Anger. What is its light? What are its virtues? Naming the positive forms of Anger will help you change how you act when challenged and harmed to enjoy positive results. Following, are positive powers of Anger. Notice how abuse and neglect take these powers away. But as you reclaim them, you heal and remove the effects of trauma.

Anger Purifies and Transforms

When Anger destroys, it makes room for something new; it changes things. When differences lead to frustrations between two people or nations and frustrations lead to fighting, know that something needs to change. Even the most positive change

166

requires "what was" to be destroyed: a stubborn unwillingness to talk, listen, give, accept, or compromise. These create conflict that will either blow the relationship up or be burned away—the process of purification. When impurities are burned away, pure gold remains. But you must be able to handle the heat.

Anger Gives You a Voice

"The pen is mightier than the sword" recognizes words as our most powerful tool to cut down or defend and protect. Your power to speak is essential! If you can't speak up, you will be someone's doormat! Finding your voice, learning to speak up, setting boundaries, saying "no," asking for what you want and saying what you feel are essential communication faculties to be learned and practiced if you're going to be free.

Anger Gives You the Power to Choose

In the direst circumstances, you may not like your choices, but you always have one. Freedom of choice is the power people die to obtain and defend. Use it early, often and practice until it becomes natural.

Anger Is Ambition

It's the fuel of conquerors, empire builders, corporate takeovers; of non-profit founders, business start-ups, change-makers, innovators and risk-takers; of skill learners and dream followers. It is the fire that forges impossible feats.

Anger Fuels Determination

It is the fire in the belly that keeps you going when things are hard, when no one believes in you, when things haven't worked out before. Use its energy to start over and try again.

Anger Gives Courage

Heroes often report that in the heat of battle, they didn't feel brave, but rather some strong force pushing them through the fear to overcome the obstacle. This force is a form of your great and glorious Anger!

Anger Teaches Empowerment

Empowerment is a higher level of power where you know who you are, what to do, what you achieve without the struggle. It brings confidence, ease, relaxation, responsiveness and effectiveness.

Anger Creates Sovereignty

When you are the master of your domain, handling what you can control, accepting and working with what you cannot, you become the autonomous Queen or King of your world, generously using resources to empower others.

Anger Brings Honor

Life is a gift. When any precious thing is defiled and despoiled, it is dishonored. In some cultures, honor was more important to defend than one's own life. When Anger is used well to protect and defend without harming, it restores honor. Your honor cannot be taken away by others; it is a personal stance. To be dignified, noble and graceful in the most wretched conditions is honor self-bestowed.

The Invincible Shield Practice for Energetic Boundaries

> "When I repress my Anger and feel I have no power, I am afraid, indecisive, don't take action. When I feel my power, I feel no fear."
> —Sarah

Past harmful experiences can leave your nervous system frayed and your more subtle energies vulnerable to the negativity of others. This simple creative visualization will do wonders to restore the habit of feeling self-contained and protected.

Begin your practice sitting still with eyes closed in a quiet place. As it becomes familiar, you can do it with eyes open along with vigorous exercise or in any other activity or challenging situations and confronting conversations.

Breathe deeply, slowly and powerfully with maximum movement in the abdomen, pushing the belly far outward as you inhale fully and pulling it all the way back against your spine as you exhale completely. Feel your solar plexus active and powerfully in control of this vital process, feeding yourself abundantly with life-giving air. Feel in total control of your breathing and your life. Spread the feelings of life, energy, strength and power throughout your body. Sit up straight and tall, expand outward all around. Cultivate feelings of your much-needed and fully deserved empowerment. You are here on earth and every life must protect and preserve itself. Feel your determination; turn it up like a light on a dimmer switch. Breathe with determination. Grow your courage; spread it from your belly out into your entire body. You are in charge of your domain. You can use all this power to be peaceful and to care for others.

Keep breathing powerfully with all these qualities surrounding you. Now imagine a protective force field completely surrounding you, an energetic shell that guards you. Make it invisible or bright, white, or any color; use your creative imagination. Start with it at least twelve inches from your skin.

Bring to mind any experiences of harm in your life and with each memory, let your Anger rise. Feel your great protective Anger radiating from the strong movements in your belly. Pump your Anger out of the abdomen and into this auric shield, using Anger to charge it up and expand it to at least three feet and up to nine feet radius from your body. Continuing with memories of harm to fuel your Anger, pump it out of the belly into the ever-increasing invincibility of your shield.

Now step back in your mind's eye to feel safe, innocent and regal inside this secure shell. Honor your precious life like the most precious diamond protected in a bulletproof case. See how relaxed you can be now, knowing you are completely safe, your boundaries respected. Inside the periphery of your body is your heart, the true queen on the throne of your being. Feel the powerful innocence at the core of your being. No matter what has happened in your life, this precious part of you is not wounded, not harmed, has suffered no loss of love. Feel the love: as much as you will allow is there for you to enjoy. It is your job to protect the sanctity of your sacred heart. And you can.

Focus again on your energetic shield. Refresh it in strength and size with your belly breath. Visualize in the far distance a past or present situation or person of threat, challenge, or harm. If the mere thought of it diminishes your sense of power and safety or the size of your aura, consciously hold the person

170

at a distance and pump your aura back up; empower yourself anew. When you are set, imagine the person, their words or actions coming from the distance, slowly closer to you. Remain in control. Let them come only as close as you can maintain your sovereign safety without shrinking. At no time may anything penetrate your shield! Stop any intruding harm at the invincible wall of your energetic boundary. Many things got through in the past that pierced your body and heart. Push all wounds of the past out. Never again!

Practice this over and over, building the strength of your shield and testing its impenetrability to attacks in private meditation, then in real-time events. You will become less reactive, less affected by the negativity of others. But this shield is not a wall; it is more like a drawbridge. You can let in anything that is safe and uplifting, anyone who supports you, any thought that empowers you, any love that fulfills you. Practice this ability to welcome in that which is right for you and filter out whatever does not serve you. Merely remembering and feeling your energetic boundary at any time or place will bring you back into your power and better able to control challenging situations to affect positive outcomes.

Ideas to Refine Your Power

Using Anger skillfully is essential to your personal well-being and contributes to world peace. Get to know it intimately and develop a strong working partnership through self-awareness, inner dialogue and outer practices like:

- Finding your voice, speaking up, making requests.
- When Anger arises, ask, "How am I using it: not at all (repressed), destructively, or constructively?"
- Learn how to create and maintain healthy boundaries. You do have to train people how to treat you. And anyone worth being in a healthy

relationship with will relearn how to treat you. But don't expect them to know: it is your job to know what is okay with you and what is not.

- Know how to say "no." If you are a pleaser, overwhelmed, or feel taken advantage of, practice saying "No." You can do it softly and kindly or with high intensity. Watch the power of your words work for you.

- If you are indecisive, look for lots of little decisions to make and make them quickly. Challenge yourself to make any decision in nine seconds or less. The human brain needs no more than that. Open the menu when the waitperson arrives and order immediately. Go to a climbing gym and move steadily upward without thinking. Go through clutter and old papers and put each item you touch in a Save, Give Away, or Trash pile within nine seconds of touching it.

- Make ten requests each day, small and large. Ask people to do things for you, give you things, do favors, say kind things to you. Even if you only get half of what you ask for, that's five new things a day. More importantly, you overcome old habits that leave you wanting.

- Learn Non-Violent Communication by Marshall Rosenberg. It will train you to do great things with your words.

- Take a public speaking or debate class. Join Toastmasters or similar group that rotates speakers.

- Practice speaking without demands or expectations, without neediness or manipulation. Be straight, direct, authentic and generous. Be the giver.

- Speak up right away when things feel off. Address

172

issues early. Speak up before irritation builds up.
- Take some martial arts training to exercise your physical strength and empowerment.

Handle Your Precious Life Well

The essential skill in working with Anger is to bring forth the full power of the beast in us and put it to work for the good of all, to consciously channel that energy to handle life with grace. If Daia can do that, recover her lost power and use it well, so can you.

> *"Since I began understanding and channeling my Anger, I have just felt happier. I realized that I'm blaming my husband and son for making me unhappy, but it's just me being angry, especially at men. My previous relationships were with men that weren't fulfilling my needs and made me angry. I stuck around because I was looking for people to blame, complain and feel negative about. All an illusion of strength, but it didn't do anything to improve my situation. It was great to realize that all my past pain and present frustrations aren't solved by just being angry. Since then, I've been able to catch my mental complaining in the moment and focus on solutions. Speaking up to my son and husband is like magic; they both treat me so well now. I can take control and at the same time, I don't have to try so hard. I am more calm and patient when I feel that I can handle life with my words." —Daia*

Chapter 8

Repair Love:
Use Grief to Heal Your Heart

> *"'Tis better to have loved and lost,*
> *than never to have loved at all."* —W. Shakespeare

Well, is it? When you are in the deep pain of Grief, agonizing the loss of that which brought light to your life and feeling robbed of the good memories that flood your mind, you might disagree. Alfred Lord Tennyson wrote "In Memoriam" while grieving the sudden loss of his good friend and saw loss as nature's cruelty. Fact is, constant change is the very nature of life. All things and experiences, family, health and life itself are all temporarily on loan: all that comes to you will someday go away. In this physical world defined by impermanence, we evolved with—and you have—an extraordinary faculty dedicated to processing loss and change.

Grief and its forms of sadness, sorrow, loneliness and regret, is the deep introspective emotion that painfully points out what you value. When something goes missing, that dull pain and emptiness in the heart is its language. It is a beautiful emotion, for when you feel it your heart is open and alive: where there is sadness there is love. If you don't care, you don't cry! As with all emotions, it can take over and take you down. But working consciously with Grief brings relief and more. Mindful use of Grief brings insight that nothing in the Universe is ever lost. You are complete and whole amidst all the comings and goings in life that pass your way.

Sarah's Sadness Subsides

"My most significant and traumatic loss was the death of my mother from breast cancer. I was 12 when I lost everything I wanted. I have held onto profound sadness and Grief all these years. Losses? Here's my list: loss of a happy childhood by growing up in a dysfunctional family, loss of security from an angry, abusive father, loss of feeling loved from a cold stepmother, loss of trust in people, loss of hope that I could be happy. I felt abandoned, alone, unloved, unworthy, invisible and inferior. I used coping mechanisms such as perfectionism, people pleasing, being over-responsible and high achieving, co-dependent in relationships, busyness, inability to express myself and my emotions...all to mask the pain I did not want to feel.

This work has shown me how to grieve and helped me feel safe to do so; I am finally beginning to heal these old wounds. From Desire, I learned self-care and from Anger protective boundaries with the people I had allowed to abuse me all these years. Stopping those re-traumatizing experiences helped heal the past and feelings of unworthiness.

In meditation, I felt dark and empty in the chest area, but as I was able to go through that, my heart felt warm and vast. I was able to sit with and then let go of the emptiness from my past losses and when I let go, amazing! I sat there with nothing but love in my heart. I have a profound experience each time I go in; the loss of my mother is becoming less painful and my memory of her is becoming more about love and security instead of deep sadness and regret. My heart now feels very open, vast and unrestricted. I feel complete and whole. I have a deep peace inside. I understand that I have everything that I need within myself and that I don't need to have to prove myself to others.

The insight I've gained from this meditation is that there's deep love in my heart and that I need to honor this love by protecting and taking good care of myself. The other significant change is realizing that all this time, I've had so much love around me. Now I want to start accepting it more into my life. Funny, actually sad, that before this healthy grieving and letting go, I was ready to leave my husband. It wasn't that he didn't love me, but that my broken heart couldn't let it in. I'm working on this and our relationship is getting better and stronger." —Sarah

Grief's Role in Healing Trauma

Sarah's mother's death was traumatic, as were the many losses that followed. Traumatic experiences involve personal loss. Count the many losses in:

Early childhood abuse: Loss of innocence, trust, security, playfulness, safe intimacy

Life-threatening accident and injury: Loss of physical ability, willingness to be in or comfort in similar situations like driving or flying, life without pain, freedom from painful memories

Divorce, death, or other endings of a relationship: Loss of love, support, companionship, pleasure, an imagined future unrealized

Losing a job or promotion: Loss of confidence, financial security, self-esteem, purpose

Realizing you aren't as young or healthy as you used to be: Diminished self-image, loss of mobility and freedom, the regret of dreams unfulfilled

Life brings loss. Grief is your psychological immune system's response to loss. As such, Grief is essential to recovery from traumatic experiences of all degrees. The essence of Grief's trauma-healing work is to make you whole again. The pain in Grief and Sadness serves to help you:

1) Clarify the things most important to you by the pain you feel when they are gone.

2) Accept the loss and let go of what was.

3) Realize how to reclaim and reintegrate into your life new forms of what was lost.

These "things lost" may be physical, like replacing a pet, home, job, or relationship. But the more profound work and healing come from using Grief to shine a light on what you need to once again feel that you are yourself: like having safety and comfort, receiving respect and love, trusting yourself and others. Loss is not always the person itself. When new relationships have a glow that fades and changes, we feel the loss of the way it was before. I'll take you through these distinctions in the upcoming exercise.

Anger and Grief are Partners in Recovery

When Anger comes online to protect you from harm, there is another part of healing that requires its partner, Grief. Every harm done to you caused you to lose something and recovery from loss is the precise job of Grief. Too often we remain angry long after trauma—even if all is safe now—when a good cry is what is needed to wash away the bitterness. Sadness is the soft but most powerful healing energy of love.

> *"While meditating with Anger, I heard the words 'I am allowed to use my anger to protect myself because I'm worth it.' I sat up much straighter and lifted my chest. I felt dignified. After the meditation some grief started to arise and I had the understanding that when Dad abandoned us and Mum didn't protect me from my stepdad, it made me feel that I wasn't worth anything. There was a huge amount of grief attached to this feeling. Much more than I knew was there." —Daia*

Trauma produces harm and creates loss. Daia's realization demonstrates how Anger and Grief each have a role in recovery. Anger is needed immediately to get you out of harm's way. Rushing to fix the wound with reconciliation and forgiveness allows the harm to continue. Grief's quiet work to heal the heart is needed later once you are safe. Daia used Anger to take back control of her life and is now ready to release the pain of lost childhood and move on to find trust and love. Staying angry about it all cannot achieve that. But the powerful feelings of Anger are too often used to mask the vulnerable feelings and healing work of Grief. So, watch for excessive Anger when Grief is calling you to heal. And watch for the avoidance of Anger that is needed to protect yourself.

To Grieve or Not To Grieve? Here's How It Goes

Unlike the bright, extrovert energies of Fear, Desire and Anger, Grief is dark, quiet and inwardly focused energy, even when it is intense. It creates conditions that call you to take time out and make space to be alone, to attend your feelings as a cat would hide and lick her wounds, to be thoughtful and introspective. Grief is bittersweet; the pain brings you to focus obsessively on what you miss, which reveals what you value. The hard but crucial work of grieving is to go through the bitter and find the sweet. As we saw earlier with Sarah, it's natural to want to avoid Grief's bitter feelings and, moreover, we just don't know what to do with them.

Failure to grieve is also a logistics problem. In any traumatic situation such as an accident, death, or divorce, there are many matters to arrange. Taking action and dealing with the physical details—medical, legal, etc. —is both urgent and necessary. To be actively doing things is often easier than wading through the thick swamp of Grief. Once affairs are handled, there will be time to heal, but often we don't want to or don't know how to go there. The feelings can lie buried for decades, quietly dulling our full embrace of life until we are ready to deal with them. So never too late to heal the heart!

The opposite of avoiding Grief is being overtaken by it. Relentless memories serve to stay with something dear while we live in a past time we prefer. A black hole in the heart swallows every joy; a piece of me is missing; my one and only source of good feelings is gone and I can't live without it. One can die of Grief, but more often, life becomes grey and joyless. Holding on to what you want is instinctual, so our first response to loss is to stay close by way of memories. To "have someone on your mind" is to have them back again with you.

Memory is so powerful and its location in the limbic system activates the same sights, sounds, smells and feelings you had then. Memories are so vivid it seems that they aren't gone at all. The same joy and happiness or other pleasures you felt are again present. You can't "get them out of your head," nor do you want to. All of this serves to slow and take control of separation. We can't bring them back, but feel an essential sense of control by holding on. And it's true: we "let go" when we are ready. Regaining this bit of power over what seems a cruel world is why grieving is a deep and individual process; we can't judge another's period of recovery. However, we can define successful, even skillful, grieving as distinct from living in prolonged sadness that will devolve into despair (see Depression, in Chapter 9.) Working well with Grief and Sadness is something anyone can learn to do.

Good Grief—Sadness Means You Care

This is how things come and go. Someone or something you enjoy comes into your life. It awakens you to new and better feelings you didn't know existed before. Once obtained, we naturally cling to these quality-of-life improvements; we want to maintain the elevated states brought to you by the thing (person, place, time, condition). We believe and fear that if the thing that made life better (brought more pleasure, joy, love, happiness) leaves, the happiness will go away too. We want to keep both. Realize that while this blessed messenger opened the doors of perception to these beautiful experiences, that door stays open for you now. Go through it to find more.

You are only sad about something you care for. Grief shows what is important to you. And what really matters is not so much the person or thing itself, but how it makes you feel. Something you love changes you; its positive effects stay with you when it is gone. Grieving is the process of recognizing what matters most and how to reclaim the experience. Here are the steps or processes of skillful grieving:

- Let the pain show you what you love.
- Through memories, feel again now all the positives about the situation. They are not lost.
- Shift your feelings from pain to the pleasure and joy of the experiences that you can feel now.
- Fully honor in gratitude the one that brought all this to your life.
- Holding to how your life has been forever enriched, accept their physical absence.
- See that you are going to be okay and let them go, while holding the love.
- Move forward to new sources of those same experiences.

When that emotional nourishment fulfills you, the sweetness is left behind. It is a gift and lasting legacy from the departed one.

A client said it so simply:

> *"Loss awakens the heart to what feeds it. Unresolved loss is painful. Resolved loss is peaceful. You have to feel it, accept it and find the goodness in it. Then, don't live in the lack of what you lost. Once you find the longing of the heart, fulfill it." —Dan*

This cycle leaves you accepting of the loss and change without being diminished by it. Life can then be a series of enhancements from each passing source that stay and accumulate throughout time. Each new, precious treasure found and added to your collection basket of life experiences fills you; there is no hole in the bottom that leaves you empty.

Love hurts, but is avoiding that pain worth the more significant loss of not loving? Make the choice to care! Reclaim your right to be boldly, beautifully sad. Honor the ability to cry. Recognize the need and the dignity of welling up and weeping for any reason. If you are a crier, own it proudly; never rush to stop or apologize. Defy the notion that it is a weakness. When you are crying your heart is open; you have an active and alive heart that feels! Let others have their discomfort with your emotional fluidity; it stems from not knowing what to do with their own feelings. And if you are a person who never cries, that's okay too. But do search inside to see if the plumbing is working, if your caring is scared and gone cold. Privately, get in touch with the richness of your heart. When you find sadness and feel moved to cry, let your heart speak to you this way. And don't just sit in that feeling: work with it! We resist this dark pain, but it wants to bring light, like this:

> *"Grief opens me up to more feeling and experiencing. It brings joy, but it makes me feel uncomfortably vulnerable; it's not easy for me to lean into it. When I do, it opens me up and brings joy." —Shiela*

Honor Your Emotional Needs

Connection, bonding, belonging, love and support are basic human needs. Getting enough is the emotional equivalent of protein and vitamins in our diet. Lack of love, *secure attachment deficiency,* has been shown to negatively affect brain development and increase physical and psychological illnesses. Love is a basic human need. But filling those emotional needs is more complicated than getting enough food and water. We may feel it is a weakness, embarrassed or undeserving and as a result, will suffer from emotional malnourishment. Just as your body lets you know when you need air and food, your heart—through sadness—lets you know when your diet is deficient in connection, love and other matters of the heart. Learn to listen and obey the longings of your heart!

> *"I've experienced much material loss in the past few years, including places and people. Learning to work WITH Grief has allowed me to move on. The harder part is to let go of beliefs like the past was better and who I thought I'm supposed to be or have by now. But realizing I am sad about how things turned out really helps me enjoy what is." —Anna*

How to Work with Grief

The traditional 7 steps of Grief are a well-known description of what most people go through after a significant loss: Shock and disbelief, Denial, Anger, Bargaining, Guilt, Depression, Acceptance and Hope. These 7 steps describe the emotions that arise when we resist Grief, inevitably succumb to reality and move on, perhaps reluctantly or begrudgingly realizinging there is no choice. But it is an ineffective misuse of the natural and highly evolved ability we have to navigate loss. There is a better way to work with this emotion.

The Essential Steps of Grieving

Here are descriptions of the steps. Following will be the same process as a guided meditation to take you through the process.

1. Sit and bring yourself to a mindful state. With eyes closed, breathe slowly and deeply while focusing

on your sensory and bodily sensations. Let the thinking mind rest.

2. Access the feelings by thoughts and memories of the loss. Let them flow, be with all the sensations. Realize you can handle this particular discomfort.

3. Feel your way through the pain to love and longing for the positive qualities, feelings and experiences that you miss.

4. Feel now those positives your heart seeks. Memory awakens those earlier feelings which live forever in you and can fill you even now.

5. Open up to see all the many ways you already have and can continue to find new sources of these same experiences. When your heart gets what it wants, you will not feel sad; you are whole again; you are healed.

6. One way to assess healing is by the degree to which the thought of that which was lost brings flourishing feelings. When life has a "net gain" and remains enhanced, you are complete and whole.

//

Exercise for Healthy Grieving—To Liberate Love

Guide yourself or someone else through Grief healing with these simple suggestions.

Sit comfortably still in a quiet place, close your eyes and breathe slowly and deeply. Pay attention to your sensations and feelings. Imagine that your breath is coming in from the center of your chest as you inhale and gently going back out from your heart area as you exhale. Continue several breaths as you relax the area and allow the breath to flow smoothly.

Let yourself feel sad. Bring to mind anyone or anything that you had and lost or wanted and didn't get. Trust that sadness reveals love and relax into the discomfort; it wants to heal, not hurt you. Be aware of sensations wherever in your body you feel them. Feel the sadness and let it flow in and out of the heart center with each breath, realizing at the same time that you are sitting here now and safe.

Have a heart-to-heart talk with yourself. See clearly who or what is the source of these feelings. What went away from you? Feel why that is so important to you. Go deeper. Turn your attention from someone or something out there inward to yourself. What did you feel and experience with and because of that which you miss? Beneath the object of your Desire, find the qualities enjoyed with it. How did you feel, or want to feel with that person or thing? Envision the experience of it and why it is so important to you. Let yourself have that experience right now through your memory and imagination of it. Focus on those positive feelings you miss and want. Breathe them in and out of the heart until your whole body fills to contentment.

The pain of loss is not from the external object, but from the internal experience. As you give that to yourself now the pain recedes, you can see more clearly now. You don't have to live without these positive feelings; they didn't come from something outside. They awakened you to that which is still inside. Is it enough that you now know what it is, how it feels and can give it to yourself? Do you still need that external prompt, or is it currently available anytime within your consciousness? When you want new sources of this experience, are they already available? Once you name the experiences your heart longs for ask it how to get more out there in your life. Envision those new sources.

Map Your Path to Recovery

Record here what you found. If the meditation didn't work for you, write about these eight steps for any loss event. One student's example is here as a prompt.

1. Identify a situation of loss/change.
"Best friends. I have had and lost so many."
Yours:

2. Name the specific thing lost and desired.
"Having someone who was always there to talk to, to share and care for one another deeply..."
Yours:

3. Describe the feelings then and now upon recalling it.
"It was like home and it felt safe. I long for that safe space, the laughter and the kinship."
Yours:

4. Now shift the focus from "it" to "you," the experience that it gave you.
"It gave me a feeling of safety, never alone, could count on someone; my heart was full from cherishing someone."
Yours:

5. Hold both as connected but separate your thoughts of the lost thing outside of you and the way it made you feel inside.
"I can see her smiling face and hear her voice while enjoying that warm feeling, then and now."
Yours:

6. Notice your enjoyment of that felt experience and that is still with you. Can you let go of that which brought you the experience and not have to lose the valuable effect they left behind in you?

"Having such a good friend really changed my life."

Yours:

7. You can still have similar experiences and feelings without that particular source. Can you identify other ways to experience those feelings?

"New friends, even if as adults we aren't always available. My spouse, to some extent. My social 'tribes' with same interests, being my own friend when I dance, exercise and spend time alone."

Yours:

8. Can you see that the power to be fulfilled and content lies with you, not with temporary external and limited things?

"I realized that a friend was 'one-stop shopping' with so many of my needs met in one place. I was just lazy and didn't want to work harder to fill their place. I was sort of pouting that I couldn't have it easy like that. That actually made me blind to all the ways my heart is filled today, actually more than back then."

Yours:

It may take some time to realize and fulfill these steps. Healing always has its own pace, with the heart as much or more than the body. Below, Sarah remained sad for many years, but this story picks up after learning how to work with Grief, when it all shifted in a month or two.

Sarah's Way Back

"My mother is gone. I miss her terribly. I think of all the family vacations, her smile, delicious meals together, being there for me whenever I was hurt. And more recently, I miss calling her on Sundays.

I tried to shift my focus from her to all the good feelings of those past times: being known, liked and cared for; feeling safe, well-fed, served with kindness, nurtured. Those good things helped make me who I am today. I can feel her lasting effect on me; she showed me how to have these feelings. Is there more of that good stuff out there for me?

What I can do for myself: Make good food at home; I have her favorite recipes. Do nice self-care things for myself the way she did for me. I can simply sit and fondly remember those sweet times, grateful for the time I had with her. That love and service is, I realize, something I give to many people.

What I can get with others: Create good times now by spending time with friends and family members. My two cats bring me a lot of affection and coziness. I'm going to start a Sunday dinner tradition of my own, a potluck with friends. I volunteer giving out food and clothes at a homeless shelter. And I want to get comfortable asking for acts of love from others. My husband started bringing me tea at night!"

—Sarah

Many Histories, Many Ways to Fill Yourself

Many people did not have this kind of loving mother. Many of our childhood caregivers inflicted loads of trauma. The sadness of *not* having those experiences can serve the same process to let go of that ideal that wasn't and the ideas of what should have been; identify your real-time current-day heart longings and needs and then create them. Positive human experiences are not indulgences: they are necessary for well-being. To experience now that which was unavailable in your past is the path to contentment. Beware the habit of settling for life without unfamiliar joys. Receiving love may take practice. Your Grief will subside as you identify what you miss or missed out on and move on. The pang of missing that special source is a way of staying connected. Enjoy it as long as you need to and let go when you are ready. You will find that by moving on from the past, the way they touched your life will always be with you.

Grief Makes Us Whole

How do we know Grief has finished its work? There are markers and measures for healing from loss. The bitter memories turn sweet. Wistful memories may come, but love is the stronger note. The net positive effect of the thing lost is appreciated, felt and stands as a life-enhancing experience. We feel whole again; nothing is missing, no black hole in the heart, life and love flow. We can enjoy life even more fully and fill the heart in many ways.

Reasons Not to Move On

Watch for these forms of resistance to letting go. They may be real, but must be accepted if you want to recover from a loss.

- I'm just not ready: Sadness has a warm embrace that in itself feels strangely comforting.
- Specialness: That was my one and only love. I'll never be like/feel like that again. Nothing else can ever replace how good it was. There is no one else for me.
- Comparing: Your dinners, hugs, way of knowing what I need just aren't as good, aren't as delicious and beautiful as theirs. It's just not the same.
- Unfaithfulness: I loved her so much it would be wrong to be happy now/love another. Moving on is a betrayal.
- It's too late: I'm too old, there's not enough time, I don't know how anymore.
- Feeling unworthy, undeserving, unlovable. No one would want me now. (More on worthiness in Chapter 11, about Shame.)

Proactive Grief Used to Release and Renew

An example of proactive Grief is called Pre-Grieving or Negative Visualzation. You do this when a person has a terminal prognosis, when you see a relationship, career, or time in your life is nearing an end, or anytime to come to peace with mortality. It is wise to contemplate and accept transitions a bit at a time and in advance. Sudden changes are always harder. In case it's not clear by now, the way to work with Grief is to let yourself feel it. In this case, go ahead and feel sad that a life—yours—will be over. Breathe through it like when you are getting some dental work done; stay present and in charge of yourself. And surrender to the truth of it. You will feel better and live in greater peace.

In this way, sadness can also serve to revive appreciation.

When the honeymoon stage of a relationship, the excitement of the outset of a career or the enthusiasm for life itself dim with time, sadness will show up. Use it sensitively to let go and be present to the beauty of what is, as it is now. This proactive response to sadness brings love and joy back to the heart without the heavier heartbreak of a breakup or complete loss to awaken recognition of what is most important to your happiness.

You can also use Grief proactively as a tool to target anything you are better off without: the drug or behavior of your addiction, a career you need to leave, a toxic relationship that is not fixable but hard to leave. Identify the thought/belief/behavior; recognize what it gave you, what purpose it served; see a new and better way; be sad to say goodbye, then let it go! We form attachments to emotional states as well as to things. Recognize when you have become strangely comfortable with chronic emotions, where you might not recognize yourself without them. Can you release them to make room for new and better feelings? Mourn the loss of familiar and once life-saving Anger, Anxiety, Depression, or sadness itself. They will always be there if you need them, but are not meant to move into your life permanently.

Nothing is Lost—The Higher Lesson of Grief

At every level, Grief teaches us to let go. And that we will not only be okay but have an even larger space in our hearts. The markers of this level of healing of the human condition are love and reverence for all things, a clear sense that there is no loss but that the Universe is always one complete whole, that there is enough out there and inside you to be made whole and complete at every moment.

When you face any loss, you confront ALL loss. Sadness creates an opportunity to come to terms with the truth of impermanence. The ego—our sense of self-preservation and self-importance—fears the fact that it is not the unique center of all things, that it is a passing fancy. This conflict between universal truth and our limited scope can be resolved in Griefwork. Spoiler alert, the only resolution is to accept this higher understanding: in the Universe, matter and energy are never lost—they continually change forms.

Whether you accept this law of physics and imagine that every atom in you is and will be once again recycled, or perceive rebirth in more esoteric fashion, or simply enjoy that every life leaves a legacy that builds on the ongoing evolution of life, there is peace in these higher perspectives. Your life is part of a vast "organism" called Universe; your existence is as brief as a snowflake and as unique and beautiful; there is enough here to fulfill you completely.

To open the door to this truth, allow Grief to open your heart and mind with its rich caring and turn your attention from one special loss to mortality itself. I say we need to grieve more—for the old days, for people we knew and places we once lived, for our lost youth, our wasted life, for simpler times in our life—so we can fully value them. Mourning the human condition could change your relationship to all losses to come, create great gratitude and reverance for every gem and crumb that comes and then leave you forever enriched by its having touched you for a moment.

Chapter 9

Reawaken Hope:
Use Depression to Start Anew

Work hard, fight strong, never give up, push through the pain, don't quit! That's how to get things done, right? But when you are depressed you don't, you won't, you can't do anything at all. In our ambitious and aggressive culture, such feelings are seen as weak and useless. Surprisingly and counter-intuitively, feeling powerless, helpless and hopeless is exactly how Depression achieves its valuable work to help you give up dysfunction and work smarter.

We are in times of constant and rapid change in human activities, thought and consciousness. When we don't know what to do with sadness, it may be mistaken for or move into depression. Currently, about 14% of Americans are on medication for depression. Although this covers only those who are actively seeking medical attention, the real toll of depression is much higher. Is there a natural wisdom at work? What is Depression trying to say and do for us?

Skillful Depression work begins with a total makeover of your ideas about and relationship to this dark and much-misunderstood emotion. Its presence means something's not working, that something about how you operate needs review and renewal. Not doing anything can sometimes achieve what pushing harder cannot. Depression brings you humbly to your knees to loosen your tight grip on old and ineffective ways. If you accept what you don't know and let things come to their overdue end, new and better ways have room to appear.

"I quit trying to get rid of depression and started trying to learn from it. I couldn't take action on my new business and cursed myself for being lazy. When I tried genuinely not caring about it all for once, I saw how much I care what my parents thought—that I am not as successful as they are, so why try at all? I got into a state of not giving a damn about anything; I thought, 'I don't care what you think!' and got free at last to be me!" —Jeremy

Please proceed cautiously with this emotion. I fully trust the healing power of Depression when it is understood, accepted and approached with mindful self-inquiry. But you must judge your readiness to do so. It's appropriate to be cautious of getting into a darkness that has been hard to escape when Depression, not you, are in control. The information and personal exploration that follows are simple and proven safe, but not tested with severe clinical depression. Know yourself well enough to decide if you can be guided by this book or need professional support to be safe. If Depression has been strong in your life, don't start here. Work with several other emotions first, so you better know your emotional landscape. Important: if you or someone you know is having suicidal thoughts, actively wishing for death, don't go it alone: get help. Go to the closest emergency room or call a suicide hotline for immediate evaluation by a medical professional.

Get Out by Going Through

Depression is not a dysfunction! But there are dysfunctional uses of Depression. Emotional liberation requires skillful use of emotions, as opposed to having them take control of us. When Depression takes over, we lose our will to act; apathy is the essence of Depression. Those deadened feelings and their effects on our lives can keep us stuck in a cycle: don't get something, get discouraged, lose energy but keep trying less effectively, still don't succeed, feel worse, harder to act. Breaking the cycle becomes more unlikely when apathy becomes a warm blanket of not feeling and not caring that protects from having to deal with life. Losing that safety means facing the world again, but that didn't go well before. Add to this the judgments that it's all shameful and weak, seen as checked out, incapable and crippled. We weakly fight it, determined not to lose, which only keeps us stuck, hanging on to the edge of an abyss unable to climb or let go.

A mental shift in approach can change the balance of power between Depression and me: a leap of faith to trust that these feelings have a purpose and choose to let go and fall. Overcoming the fear of this kind of falling is like finding the courage it takes to jump out of a plane skydiving based on trust in the parachute and the whole skydiving system. None of us ever learned to trust emotions and therefore haven't seen evidence that there is safety built into this system of emotions. To believe I won't die, but that I let something in my life die, fall away and leave me free.

Grief and Depression

Being sad about loss and death is appropriate and quite different from being depressed about it. Grief is commonly mistaken for Depression. They share similar low energy states and introspective focus, but their purpose differs. Knowing the difference equips you to deal with them appropriately. Where Grief helps you let go of what has already gone (see previous chapter, on Grief), Depression shows where you refuse to accept a past or pending loss. Where Grief sends us into the heart to recognize love, Depression goes deeper to confront our beliefs, purpose and very existence. Depression sufferers

195

may have some unaddressed grieving to do in addition to their renewal work. Without that, sadness can descend into Depression. Resisting inevitable loss leaves us incomplete and can make the whole world seem cruel and against us; this is a mental recipe for Depression.

Depression is complicated and challenging to deal with; it is nonetheless possible that its solutions are simple, if not easy. You might see valid motives: a need for the shelter of aloneness, space to understand and make peace with yourself, to hide when you don't know what to do. You may require a break from "normal" to gain strength, even if others view your apathy with sympathy. Our approach in Emotional Liberation is that disturbing emotions arise to resolve problems—as antibodies in your psychological immune system. Depression shows up when the pathway through a situation calls for you to stop and make changes. It calls for in-depth work on the physical and mental foundations of your behavior. I have seen it work wonders, like this:

Lisa Lets Go of Poor Self-Image

"I suffered a lot of early relational trauma. My adult life saw brilliance and success, but persistent anxiety brought periods of withdrawal from it all. I was depressed for years, went on and off medication and through various therapies. It seemed that my brain chemistry meant a lifetime curse of going nowhere. In one cycle of really heavy depression, I hit a new low. Ready to give up on everything, it came to me sadly in a therapy session, 'I have no purpose.' My therapist said, 'You'd be a wonderful therapist.' She and many others had told me this over the years. The

*same sensitivity that makes life hard makes me
an insightful listener. At that moment, my fears
and inadequacies dropped away, leaving a new
idea of helping people—and having a life! My
energy and willingness to TRY came back.
Within two weeks, I found and enrolled in a
Master's program. My anxiety is there, but
isn't stopping me now. I had built a story out
of my fears and failures that I was incapable of
success and happiness. In that state of totally
giving up, I dropped that self-image in favor of
a new identity, helping others who suffer as I
have. To move ahead, I also had to let go of
earlier ideas of what I should do and be in life,
which held me believing myself a failure."* —
Lisa

Fear of the Dark

We are naturally scared of the dark, of the unknown, of
emptiness, a nothingness which feels instinctively unsafe. But
these are the very qualities of Depression that have beauty and
purpose we can discover and use. By learning to find trust and
peace rather than dread in things beyond our comfort zone,
understanding, or control, we can receive the benefits that
Depression offers. Quite counter-intuitively, Depression takes
us into the dark to find safety there. It cuts off the will to hold
tight to the thing we must give up to move again.

Accepting Lows and Highs

The cycle of existence includes Birth, Growth, Decline,
Death, Rebirth. Beginnings are more beautiful and fun, while
endings seem sad. We naturally seek the lighter side of life,

but you can't have one without the others. Whether it's a physical thing, a business, a relationship, or an idea, everything comes and goes. What a crowded and boring world if nothing died. The old goes away to make way for the new and improved. We cling to what we have and know, while resisting the unknowns that come with change. Desiring the creation of new things without allowing the old to fall away is to work against the way of the world—that's a fight no one can win. Nature will bring you to your knees to teach this lesson, or you can learn to accept and feel safe with the dark side by visiting and getting to know it by feeling it in your body, somatically.

/ /

Experience your preference for the growth side of the life cycle. Recite slowly and feel your response to these words.

Deterred	Despondent
Derailed	Despairing
Discouraged	Depressed
Descend	Destruction
Decline	Decay
Deteriorate	Death

What a downer, right? The prefix "de" comes from Latin, meaning "down."

New life of some kind always follows death; rebirth is part of the cycle. Now feel your visceral responses as you slowly read these words. The prefix "re" means "again'.

Relax	Recover
Release	Restore
Rest	Revive
Relieve	Renew

Refresh	Reframe
Replenish	Reimagine
Revitalize	Recreate
Reinvigorate	Reconstruct
Rejuvenate	Resurrect
Reset	Reborn

If you trust that every down opens the way to something new to come again, you can accept and appreciate—maybe enjoy—both sides of life. Imagine Depression as the battleground between our small egos' agenda and the unstoppable ways of the world. Pat said it well:

> "In my meditation with depression, I saw myself clinging to a vine over the rushing river of my current fears. Then it occurred to me how nice it might be to relax, let go and drop into the rapids, into whatever might happen, fears and all. I took that approach back to my stalled attempts to change careers and things started to move." —Pat

Trauma and the Cycle of Depression

Feeling trapped increases trauma. We feel helpless when there is nothing we can do to get out of danger, like being pinned in a wrecked vehicle or forcefully held down. We feel hopeless when stuck in a long-term situation with no way out, like growing up in an abusive or neglectful family. Feeling powerless, helpless and hopeless create Depression, which, in turn, creates thoughts and behaviors that work against you. You won't take the actions needed to get out of trouble. Lethargy and fatigue, apathy, not caring, not trying, giving up, seeing no way out all keep us stuck. Thus, Depression makes trauma recovery harder. But its purpose is to slough off dead parts of ourselves so our better life can rise.

Depression is rarely the "first responder" to a disaster. Terror (Fear), fighting back (Anger), blaming oneself (Guilt and Shame) and mourning (Grief) arise immediately to warn, protect, restore dignity and to heal. When these problematic emotions relentlessly persist, numbness, dissociation and other forms of withdrawal are a natural protective recourse. When the higher energy emotions like Anger and Fear don't help a situation, either because we don't know how to work with them or the situation is just too overpowering, Depression sets in. We are like a tortoise pulling into its shell.

But when circumstances are favorable for an escape and a change, we must return to feeling and acting to save ourselves. Healing trauma requires an ability to face and deal with the many emotions that seek to help you. Each has a specific role to play in the cleanup. Despair feels like a dark pit; use it as a pit stop. Take a break from the race to rest and repair. Those repairs include updating historical thinking and previously life-saving but now limiting coping strategies. When refreshed, you can get back out there.

Digging Into the Roots of Depression

How does Depression start? The protective emotions all have an inception point and then develop patterns with time—all in their efforts to help. In chronic and developmental trauma, they are milder at first but intensify from the repetition of the harm. In acute trauma, they burst forth immediately with intensity. If emotions achieve getting you back to well-being, they recede. If not, they stick around until they complete their work, becoming more substantial and more pervasive just as toothache pain increases until you deal with it. Persistent emotions are a sure sign of unresolved issues and facing them is the shortest path to relief. But when first responder emotions don't succeed, Depression is your system's back-up plan. The effect is a loss of energy and hopelessness in a bid to achieve through no energy what hasn't worked by way of high-energy responses. When trapped in adversity, "There's nothing I can do," may be the immediate response. In either case, working with Depression will invariably uncover a cloud of the other protective emotions that all have a valuable role to contribute to a successful return to well-being.

It's time to take a dive into these special dark feelings. At this point your response is likely either trepidation to go there, or "No problem, that's not an issue for me." If the first applies, we do need to look at the wound if we are to heal it, but only when you feel safe and ready. If you've never related to Depression, I bet it can help you to get to know its healthy resorative power. For you, sit slouched forward and hang your head using the body language of exhaustion and defeat and breathe weakly as you contemplate the following questions.

Remember your earliest thoughts like, "I can't do it; there's no way; it will never happen."

> What was happening that brought you to think that way?
> Remember all the feelings. Was there frustration? List all other emotions you felt.
> What were you wanting and what was in your way?
> Was someone or something huge and powerful stopping you or pushing you?
> How did you go about the efforts you made?
> Did you ask for help?

Was it unreasonable to expect you could do it?

Were you impatient, demanding, unwilling to accept alternatives?

Did you give up easily or fight on too long?

Who were your role models and how did they go about getting things done?

What were the socio-economic and political conditions: a depressed economy, controlling governments, oppressive parents, limitation of personal freedoms?

//

Your experiences and environments shaped your beliefs about what is possible or not, your sense of empowerment and possibility. They, in turn, determine how easy or hard it seems to get money, find love, take on challenges. It's your story: see it as just a story, one that you haven't finished. You can determine where it goes from here, no matter what has happened so far. You will likely see similar experiences, feelings and results from your past recurring in your present life—your patterns. It's all a story we tell ourselves with entrenched neural pathways in the brain that fire automatically in familiar territory. But these thought/feeling/ behavior habits are like the thermostat in your home heating system: you can reset them!

Now take at least an equal amount of time to rewrite your story. You have heard lots of advice, mottos and words of encouragement that you may have written and repeated to inspire more hope, enthusiasm and energy. Did it work? Did it stick? Positive thinking may not overcome subconscious beliefs. Replacing those takes more self-awareness and a new approach. Depression is all about the limits of pushing, trying, fighting and resisting. It brings us to confront our limits honestly and embrace a new way.

"Under heaven, nothing is more soft and yielding than water. Yet for attacking the solid and strong, nothing is better."
—The Tao Te Ching

Discover the gifts of darkness. It is peaceful, still, quiet, tranquil. Without it, you can never rest. Doing nothing invites relaxation, thinking nothing brings sleep, being empty makes room to be filled. It is the space that makes a cup useful. There must be emptiness for something to have a place to go. An empty mind is a peaceful one. Everything needs space to grow. You must let go of this breath before you can take the next one. In a fast-moving car, you must slow down to turn around. Can you sit and do nothing, or is staying busy more comfortable? Can you wait for love and projects to grow, or must you always go on the hunt and push an agenda like "real winners" do?

The Art of Empowered Surrender

Depression comes when change is needed. The improvement I need has no room in my life until I drop an older way of thinking and doing things. But what will happen if I let go of what I know has helped me survive so far? When is it better to fight on with familiar defenses, or take up new ones, or give up and walk away from the whole thing? Prevailing Western values see surrender as cowardly and giving up as a failure. In Eastern philosophies, surrendering can be a powerful choice, submitting to rise higher, bowing to honor and gain access to something greater, being humble as an act of wisdom. One way to work with Depression is to ask, "What must I drop to get unstuck?" The ancient sage Lao Tsu wrote about the value accomplished by letting things go their course. To help familiarize you with this different mindset, I have paired some of his lines with excerpts from personal growth stories of Emotional Liberation practitioners.

Darkness within darkness, the gate to all mystery.

"It was painful, but I see that I had to go low to get to a better place."

The sage is detached, thus at one with all.

"When I gave up always having to be right, we started getting along again."

Shape clay into a vessel; it is the empty space that makes it useful.

"Our long-term relationship was almost dead until I quit working all the time. We started to spend some time just hanging out together and I realized he really does care about me."

Everyone else is busy, but I alone am aimless and depressed. I am different; my great mother nourishes me.

"I did the corporate sales game and burned out. Depressed that I had failed, it finally dawned that I was pursuing someone else's dream of success. I always wanted to be a counselor and am now studying to do that—content at last."

He who strides cannot maintain the pace.

"I thought happiness meant I should always be positive and energetic but see that my flow of up and down energies are natural and healthy."

Retire when the work is done, this is the way of Heaven.

"I was constantly frustrated with my kids; always nagging them to do things better (my way!). I gave up being the perfect parent. We're all happier now."

The sage is guided by what he feels. He lets go of this and chooses that.

"I quit trying so hard to improve myself and started caring for myself. Big difference!

Empty yourself of everything; let your mind rest at peace.

I'd been fighting clutter for years. I just can't do it anymore. When I switched my thinking from de-cluttering to creating harmony around me, peace returned to my home."

Surrender yourself humbly; then, you can care for all things.

"When I feel frustrated and stuck, now I stop to meditate; I get calm and am more productive afterward."

The highest good is like water; it gives life to all and does not strive.

"Spirituality saved my life, but in recent years I am miserable again. I have been holding some ideal of what I should be and do to be 'good.' It's a relief to let that go now and just be me. I am enough!"

Your Turn

Write about how you can apply this next Taoist truth spiritually and practically to your life to give you more room to breathe and space to live.

Yield and overcome; Bend and be straight; Empty and be full; Wear out and be new; Have little and gain; Have much and be confused. Be really whole and all things will come to you.[3]

Giving Up Is Hard to Do

I remember an old movie in which the bad guy is hanging off a cliff with one hand up clutching the edge. His other hand is down, holding tightly to a heavy bag of gold. He doesn't want to die, but he has spent years dreaming of, planning for, then getting that gold. Now he has it and is very attached to it and all that it means. He can't let go of all his ideas about his life with gold, so he can't let go of the bag. Yes, he drops to his death and loses both. Holding on happens at the group and institutional levels as well: environmental calamity is a global example of how difficult it is for us to change even when current ways are failing. What causes us not to let go of things

---

[3] Sections above adapted from *The Tao Te Ching* of Lao Tsu, translation by Gia Fu-Feng and Jane English.

that aren't serving us might not be greed, but rather survival instincts, habits and sticking to what we know. We need something and don't know a better way to go about it. It may seem counter-intuitive to go further into the darkness to find the light, but how well has hanging on to the edge of the abyss worked? It can be evident to you that others need to drop old ways and change because you are not in their story, nor are you attached to it. For the same reasons, it is harder to see your own. Friends and counselors often try to help us understand.

Find What You are Holding On To

Ask yourself these questions. Your answers will prepare you for the meditation to follow.

- When has holding on to something hurt you?
- Are you holding grudges, operating on outdated beliefs, sticking to old habits, going along with what others expect, how parents did things, unsatisfying work, or toxic relationships?
- What changes are you resisting? You might see the signs in depression, frustration, confusion, fear, desperate attempts to convince or attack others' views.
- Are you willing to look at new ways and test them?
- When is giving up the best way to win?
- Can you let others be right and validate their ways of thinking and doing? Or do you create dis-harmony in relationships by sticking hard to and forcing your views? You don't have to agree, but can you try to hear and imagine how they see it?
- How can giving up help you find a way through a

block? How do you know what to give up on and when?

Your mind may be confused, but in your gut, you know. The skill is to listen. Here's a practice in the healthy use of surrender as a choice to find a better way.

Letting Go to Make Room for Something New

Sit comfortably in a quiet place and become still. Breathe slowly. You'll get the best results by breathing four times per minute. Count to a ticking clock, taking 8 seconds to inhale fully and 8 seconds to exhale completely. If this is too difficult, start with a smaller number with steady, equal in-and-out movements. Continue for five minutes or longer until you feel an increase in your peacefulness.

Think of a bothersome issue, one in which that you feel stuck: financial fears, physical ailments, relationship issues with someone, news events, global warming, etc. Focus on the thoughts and feelings you have about this; watch them churn and swirl. Get sick and tired of the whole thing. Don't care. Give up. Let it all blow up and go away. Let it die.

Move away from effort and energy toward softness. Let your body go limp. Quit trying. Don't care about it all. Let your whole being be free of the turmoil. Empty yourself. Relax into nothingness. Float in deep space where it's quiet, rest in peace. You may feel sadness, resistance, attachments and have good reasons not to let go. Reassure yourself. Try trusting. Enjoy the lack of struggle.

When you are genuinely carefree, new ways of seeing and dealing with the issue will arise. Don't get excited or attached to any single idea. Let your wise inner eye look down from space on this issue with a fresh perspective. Remain nicely detached; let your body, not your mind, feel for new answers. Don't try to figure anything out. Don't push. Patiently sit, ready to listen if answers do come.

What is really happening?

What is it you want?

Is it so important? Would something else do?

Is there another way you hadn't seen?

What is in your way?

Remember the bandit who couldn't let go of his gold to save himself? What are you holding on to? Old goals, poor self-images, false limitations, outdated dreams, expectations, beliefs, stories of earlier failures, bad habits, fears?

Seeing any, let them go. Release.

What is it like without all that?

Now, patiently wait without any agenda to see what might arise and appear in the space you have created. Let answers come if they will. And when they do, surrender to them. Trust your inner vision when it is clear and unattached to the past.

Do you yet see some hope?

When you are content with the process, slowly come back into the present and open your eyes. Write about your experience. Will you follow through on something you see that is needed, even if it is new and uncomfortable? Short-term discomfort to make a change will leave you happier in the long term.

It is natural to want things and we want them now! Impatience to get them and lack of trust in what comes to us and when, can create a loss of hope and the motivation it gives us to keep trying. Hopeful or hopeless, powerful or powerless, helpful or helpless are all thoughts. In Depression, the 'less' thoughts ensnare us: the mind cannot reach the "full" thoughts. Dropping all thoughts in meditation, learning to be present and mindful to immediate reality over tightly held imaginings is another way to use the wisdom of apathy.

Ironically, that does take some effort to learn control of the mind's wandering and decide to let dark thoughts go dark.

Depression under Pressure

Another form of resistance to Depression is to push harder, to run away from its mission. Call it "hyper-depression" or "cold depression." Instead of slowing down to turn around, we push harder, over-stimulate, hang on for dear life and keep running away from feelings and situations we don't want to address. In our demanding and driven 24/7 culture, being busy is expected and always viewed as positive, while taking time out is seen as unambitious, weak and getting behind the competition. Covering fear of our dark side with distracting action further buries the self-reflection and correction Depression requires of us.

> *"Because I suffered from cold depression, I can't say enough about the importance of recognizing it. When I began this work and we listed what we thought were our top difficult emotions, I dismissed Depression because of my stereotypical assumption that depression is going into a fog and doing nothing. I realize now I was depressed but, instead of shutting down in despair, I went hyper to try out-running it and not feeling that awful darkness. I was in such a state of Shame that I couldn't allow myself to go inward to look at myself and release my negative self-image. Instead, I charged outward, pushing hard to prove myself in a futile effort to gain acceptance and validation. It took two years of work to unravel all that. I now see it's as common a condition in*

our culture as the traditional picture of Depression." —Becca

Depression Begs for Rest

Rest and rejuvenation are changes that Depression demands. In these fast-moving times, being too busy, overwhelmed, over-stimulated and exhausted are the norm. The "global epidemic of depression" can be understood as a natural response to mitigate out-of-control stress, a symptom of and solution to overloaded nerves, thoughts and other emotions. Underlying Depression are often other neglected emotions lying in wait to do their work. When high-energy pushing from Fear, Desire and Anger don't succeed, it is "plan B," helping us discover the power of not doing, allowing, waiting and patience. These are the woefully under-appreciated yin (feminine) counterparts to the yang (masculine) energies and approaches that have mistakenly been considered the only types of power in our male-dominated culture.

Liz Lets Life In

"I didn't realize that I have been depressed most of my life! I covered it with busy-ness because I didn't want to face my feelings of childhood abandonment. Being overwhelmed with too much to do is like a life vest, the same as my mother used. When you had me meditate, I felt fear not to be busy. I realized how totally exhausted I am all the time. When I allowed myself to feel fed up with it, depression really hit. With professional support, calming meditative techniques and this perspective that

depression was coming to bring much-needed relief, I felt safe. I had the courage to dip into my feelings of depression. That opened doors to see my patterns clearly and how it all started. Anger at my family's mistreatment surfaced. It feels great to validate the feelings they shamed me for. How quickly I started enjoying being cozy in my home for the first time and I'm lightening my workload to leave time to enjoy myself." —Liz

Balance Your Energy Account

Your life force is more precious than money. Do you operate on a balanced budget, overdraft your account, or are you already bankrupt? Depression may be showing you a way to correct the depletion of physical, mental and spiritual resources. Do you recognize these patterns in yourself or others? The first shows a spiral of diminishing effectiveness and energy. The second reacts to failure by pushing ever harder with increasing desperation. In both, something needs to stop so change can happen.

Low Energy Depression Spiral

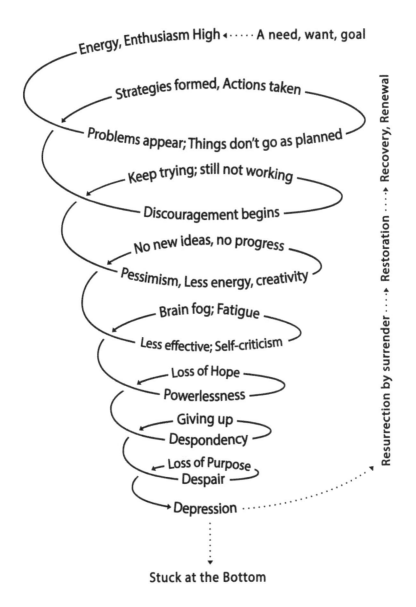

Energy, Enthusiasm High ⟵ ····· A need, want, goal

Strategies formed, Actions taken

Problems appear; Things don't go as planned

Keep trying; still not working

Discouragement begins

No new ideas, no progress

Pessimism, Less energy, creativity

Brain fog; Fatigue

Less effective; Self-criticism

Loss of Hope

Powerlessness

Giving up

Despondency

Loss of Purpose

Despair

Depression ·········

Resurrection by surrender ····▶ Restoration ····▶ Recovery, Renewal

Stuck at the Bottom

High Energy Depression Spiral

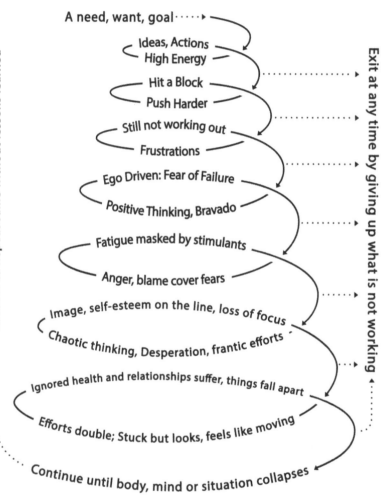

A need, want, goal

Ideas, Actions
High Energy

Hit a Block

Push Harder

Still not working out

Frustrations

Ego Driven: Fear of Failure

Positive Thinking, Bravado

Fatigue masked by stimulants

Anger, blame cover fears

Image, self-esteem on the line, loss of focus

Chaotic thinking, Desperation, frantic efforts

Ignored health and relationships suffer, things fall apart

Efforts double; Stuck but looks, feels like moving

Continue until body, mind or situation collapses

Recover to Repeat same without lessons learned

Exit at any time by giving up what is not working

A low-energy spiral goes like this:

1-Something not working needs to change

2-Same strategies and efforts don't work

3-No change

4-Don't know how or can't face the change

5-Get discouraged, lose hope, give up

6-Change is more unlikely

7-Despair deepens into a stagnant depression

Here is the high-energy cycle of "busy" depression:

1-Something not working needs to change

2-Efforts don't succeed (efforts may be avoidance, not directed at the problem)

3-No change

4- Can't accept "failure," cover fears by pushing harder with unchanged strategy or at unrelated issues to not feel powerless

5- Get tired, ignore it and increase the stimulation to keep running

6-Get same non-results

7-Repeat until something falls apart

Is this latter pattern you, using only high-energy responses to challenges? Is it working? How can you get off the treadmill? A change at any point in the cycle will work. Here are alternatives to the first four steps that will break the cycle.

1. When things fail, accept that change is needed. Be willing.
2. When efforts don't succeed, stop, relax, review the goal and the approach early. Get help.
3. When rested, continue with the clarity that you are on track and need to keep going, or
4. Give up—change something about the goal or try a

new approach that may work better.

Manage your energy as you might manage your money well. With the "income" of your resources, assess and be realistic about the time, energy, etc. you have. That may be more or less than others but can make a great life by accepting them gratefully. Don't let comparing and competing take you down. With your "expenses," don't live beyond your means. Know what is most important in your overall "budget" and spend your energy there first. You might need to cut out people and projects that drain you or can wait. And save some for later. I can tell you that as you age, your energy deposits aren't replenished as quickly.

Suggestions

- Take a Radical Sabbatical. Take a year off. Sound crazy? If your life depended on it (and it might), you would find a way. How about a year in which you do less, worry less, play more, quit trying so hard, practice contentment. A month? A week?
- Try Power Napping. Set a timer for 15 to 20 minutes and see if you can fall asleep before it gently rings. Calms the nervous system; teaches you to relax; rejuvenates. Einstein did it!
- Goldilocks' Assessment of Resources: Too much, too little, or just right? Make a list of your life's resources to balance: time, energy, money, health, food, weight, opportunities, responsibilities, motivation, ambition, ideas, pleasure, enjoyment, love, support...and so on. Next to each word, write "+" if you have too much, "-"if too little and "=" if just right. Make a simple plan of how to bring each into balance and harmony.

"I took your suggestion to sit and meditate with my depression each day for my profound fatigue. At first, I was very uncomfortable: I felt guilty for being unproductive. I judge my depression very negatively, feel ashamed of it. So, when you asked me to sit and let myself feel apathy, I was itchy. Then I saw that resisting it keeps it in place. I got quiet enough to see how exhausted I am. Back when I was in a bad relationship and didn't know what to do, I didn't want to feel and couldn't deal with it. Being busy saved me then, but not now. And in that space of quiet reflection I saw the real problem, how I please and appease people. I don't speak up with my boss or boyfriend, afraid they'll be mad at me. I'm ready to drop being a conflict-avoiding people-pleaser! It's so great to quit trying to get rid of low feelings and learn from them instead. I can now meet Depression as a friend." —Uma

Hope Springs

The Universe is made of opposites that ultimately balance each other. Night is balanced by day and the dawning of hope and optimism can follow any dark night of the soul. When you are willing to go into the cave to face Depression, you will discover its lessons and gifts. Trauma is an ugly business that steals the power, hope and the will to overcome. Making heroic efforts in the struggle to recover from harm is only half of the game. They must be complemented, balanced and fulfilled with letting things fall away. Our neurotic reactions are not lovely to look at, not our proudest moments. But we humans are built to learn from pain, to adapt to hardship and innovate ever better ways of doing and being. It is noble work that will bring you back home.

You are both powerful and powerless. What is the wisdom in being powerless? There is a power higher than you, available to you. Ego says you are all alone and must do it yourself, but can't. We may feel small in dealing with life, but all the while great forces like gravity and nuclear fusion explosions in the sun produce what we need to exist. Is it depressing to know you are a mere speck in the grand dance of the Universe? Instead of giving up, it's possible to "give it over"; let the Universe, God, destiny—however you imagine power beyond your own—take care of it. It can be completely relaxing to let the Universe spin as you watch life's ups and downs like a great movie.

Chapter 10

Recover Innocence:
Use Guilt to Clear Inner Conflict

You're caught! They found out what you did, or you're afraid they will. How does it feel? A sinking feeling in your gut? A cold shrinking feeling all over? Or you are on the other side: you can't believe they would do such a thing. Fingers point and heads shake, faces are stern. You're bad! Then, punishment. Were you hit; sent away alone; were privileges, things or love taken away? Did you become the punisher? What is your history with Guilt?

Our instincts are to get along with our tribe, not to be at odds with anyone in power. But we have another side that needs things and acts on impulse to grab what we want. These two forces stand in opposition and confuse the question, "How shall I act?" On one shoulder is my "conscience"—an "angel"—and on the other is the devil. Both sound convincing, but ultimately one of those voices will make my choice. Then come the consequences of my actions. Do I like how it all turns out?

Guilt is an internal guidance system meant to guide you toward choices that are best for you. It's an internal judge for the many conflicting voices that complicate and confuse, with an eye on consequences beyond a momentary urge. Used well, it aligns needs and actions with deeper values to keep you on your path, feeling proud. When you know who you are and behave accordingly, that is called integrity, the stuff that lets you sleep well at night. When we say, "Sleep like a baby," we acknowledge a craving for innocence and how it simplifies and makes everything easier than living in all the tangled webs we weave. Guilt is a vigilant guide ready to bring us back to that original state that Jesus taught is a hall pass to heaven.

This urge, be it to stay out of trouble or be at peace with oneself, is so powerful it can be used to control and manipulate others rather than regulate ourselves. When you don't know your truth, you can be exploited, led astray believing you are wrong and obeying the ways of others. Guilt-work reclaims your ability to know what's right for you and live to that truth, even when all that you stand for is challenged. I have had several big life-defining showdowns between what I felt I must do and what others wanted me to do. They are never easy. They forced me to dig deep and find out who I really am, what I stand for. How did it go for you?

> *"My early guilt started when my parents made me do something I didn't want to do. I would fight back fiercely, yell and refuse. When my brother held me down, I would later hit him so hard he'd cry. When my ex treated me badly, I'd hold it in—to be a good wife—until periodically blasting him with fury, later, tantrums with my daughter. I always felt guilty about how much I hurt them. I rationalized that they deserved it. I hated myself for hurting these loved ones but I couldn't stop. I blamed myself for the divorce that followed.*
>
> *Over time, I learned to say how I felt earlier to stop being hurt, got better at avoiding drama. I am proud of myself now. Guilt showed me I didn't like hurting people, showed me a better way. I guess I had to go through all that to learn how to take care of myself.*

And that thing where my ex and all our friends blamed me for the divorce, for years I believed the story that it was my fault. But realizing the courage it took to get out of his emotional abuse, I am now the heroine of the story! I know what is right." —Becky

A Tale of Two Stories

A client shared the voices she heard in her head when meditating:

> *"I should be nice to her; I hate her for what she did. I need a raise; it's selfish to ask for things; people with lots of money are bad. I'm bad to want sex; being a virgin is lame. I want to be attractive; attractive women are bimbos. Good people help strangers; all strangers are dangerous. Nice girls don't get tattoos; cool people have tattoos. Something's wrong if you're not in a relationship and have children; relationships and parenting are a nightmare. Stupid people eat junk food; I love junk food."*
> *—Shelly*

We can imagine where those opposing thoughts came from. Guilt is always a conflict between two or more stories, as between prosecutor and the defense in a murder trial, two people assigning blame in a traffic accident or a bitter divorce settlement. Who is right; who is wrong? For Becky, there was her ex's story of blame versus her truth of escaping abuse. Guilt shows up to arbitrate the tug-of-war within your heart and mind so you can stand firm on your own ground. Here's another common war of wills—whose life is it?

"My father is a powerful and selfish man. But at six, when my mother died, he fell apart and made me take care of him. To keep my source of security functioning, there was no room for me to have a life. Decades later, I would still neglect myself and run when he called. Exhaustion and resentment didn't break his power over me. But as I began to understand how he used guilt to manipulate me, I recognized that I have my own life-story, but my guilt kept me living in his. Mindful guilt showed me how to break free from that over-responsibility with him, with my husband and at work." —S.M.

People devoted to different beliefs have been at odds throughout time. When the religious kill, it's God's will; governments punish protesters under the law, parents abuse children and call it good discipline. Both sides justify their actions with story, a "truth," that says, "I am right, you are wrong." But laws and rules that claim truth change over time; what was once right is now wrong. Slavery, the stoning of adulterers and illegal homosexuality were once the law—and in some form are still not universally agreed upon, but laws and norms do evolve. Are there no absolute truths? All people get that certain feeling, better when we are right, worse when wrong. We have free will to do what's best in the moment and for ourselves, or for the future and for the group. Instinct first says "me, now!" Being social animals, we evolved more sophisticated instincts to evaluate how a choice affects our standing with others. That clash of values, of what is best and most important, is our special sense called Guilt. It's meant to help us sort through rivaling truths and find our own.

Get to Know Guilt

To use Guilt well as a tool, we need to understand how it is misused as a weapon against us and against ourselves. We'll start with the vocabulary of 'old school' Guilt. As you read these words, feel your reactions and recall any memories they evoke.

The Law	Disgrace
Crime	Dishonor
Bad	Regret
Punishment	Remorse
Justice	Sinful
Liable	Stigma
Secrets	Shame
Judged	Blame
Lies	Contrition
Wrong	Delinquent
Disobey	Fault
Accused	Misbehave
Condemned	Wrong
Redemption	Wicked

What is your history with guilt? Was it used to control you? Did you have a hard time knowing who to listen to and believe? What did you do with guilty feelings, obey or ignore them, live with or resolve them? As with all emotions, resistance breeds persistence. To get it working for rather than against you, see the pervasiveness of the old Guilt paradigm. In the pairs below, notice how the language of Guilt is based on polarities or opposites that separate everything into two simple, separate and opposing sides, only one of which can win while the other must lose. I have added an example of a more neutral or inclusive view of the bifurcated pair: it looks past either/or mentality to see people as having many sides.

Language of Duality and Exclusion	→	Language of Mutuality and Inclusion
Right/Wrong	→	Imperfect
Winner/Loser	→	In the game
Virgin/Slut	→	Woman in charge of her sexuality
Big boy/Sissy	→	Many ways to be a man
Saint/Sinner	→	Human being
Angel/Devil	→	God is everything
Righteous/Evil	→	Behavior has consequences
Gay/Straight	→	Love is a spectrum
Black Race/White Race	→	Diverse physical characteristics
Right Wing/Left Wing	→	Conviction of values
Native/Immigrant	→	People want a safe home

A narrow and polarized consciousness is embedded in our systems of justice, religion, morals and deep into our nervous systems. Concepts of God reflected this thinking: religions and mythologies explained natural disasters, famine, plague and hardship as the wrath of angry gods, punishing people for their sins. It is a linear, zero sum paradigm that operates in us today: only one thing can be right and all else is wrong, one person is good and the other bad. When a lion kills a deer to feed her cubs, is the lion bad? To the deer, yes. To her pride she is a good mother. When limited by a model of I am/you are wrong, someone must lose and must pay. The result is the cultural polarization that is increasing, or at least more visible. Each side believes they are right and the other side is wrong. In duality, no one wins. We've come from counting on fingers to supercomputers, but our Guilt consciousness has not evolved as far.

Better Beliefs

We need to install a Guilt upgrade in our operating system. Every story is an expression of the beliefs of the storyteller. And those stories create beliefs in the listener. When people were told that disease was punishment by an angry God for their sins, they felt guilty. What behavior did the teller want them to do and not do? When your mother's praise for your sister, her marriage, kids, or job feels like a punch in the gut, what does she believe will make you a "good daughter"? Both tellers share a paradigm:

> I know what is right, you don't. I am right, you are wrong.
> There is only one way, mine!
> I want you to do what I want you to do.
> I want you to think the way I do.
> There is a reward to agree and obey and a punishment when you don't.
> I can control you.

Today, when a serious virus outbreak is not contained, we are more likely to blame the government and health officials' ineptitude than an angry God. A modern woman may more likely think her mother is old fashioned and just doesn't get her, than live out what may be her parent's fears. What beliefs underlie this way of thinking?

Nothing is good or bad, but one's thinking makes it so (with thanks to W. Shakespeare).

There are many ways to go; my choices are mine to make.

I know what is right for me, or will risk making mistakes to learn.

I take responsibility for the consequences of my choices

I control my life, you control yours.

Cause and Effect

Does this mean that anything goes, nothing matters and everything is random? No, even chaos theory states that within the apparent randomness of chaotic complex systems, there are underlying patterns. In addition to the belief that our fortunes are tied to pleasing the gods, other ideas developed from observations that what happens now is connected to what happened before. In physics, it is Newton's 3rd Law: Every action in nature has an equal and opposite reaction. In Eastern philosophy it is the Law of Karma. While widely misunderstood, it simply describes cause and effect, that every action will cause a reaction in a continual chain of events. The chain goes back to the big bang: what's happening to you now is connected to everything since birth and before. The chain of events continue: what you do now shapes your future. Within the complex uncontrollable forces of nature, this gives us some control of our destiny. Once we know or can guess the effect of an action, we can modify it for a better outcome.

This is an empowering idea. It means we can control to some extent what happens to us by the actions we choose. It also means we must take responsibility; it means an end to the blame game. You may not have been able to control your parents' abuses as a child, but as an adult you have choices now. And you can choose what to do next, pass on the abuse to others, have it ruin your marriage, or find a way to affect a better future. Understanding past causes for your current situation and the consequences of what you do with it now, is a "get-out-of-jail" pass to a future free of past harm. A better belief about "Why bad things happen to good people" requires a more proactive, less punishment-seeking question: "What can we learn from harmful things about how to create life-affirming things?" Rather than "being a victim," I learn how to avoid harm next time.

Nature as Teacher

As imperfect beings we make mistakes in this imperfect world—and it's all perfect. Random genetic mutations create some species that die out while others, like jellyfish and sharks are doing well 500 million years later. Nature experiments to see what might work. Flightless birds were worth a try, but there aren't many left. Is human behavior so different? I thought I could sneak out in my parents' car at 14 and not get caught; I learned! Haven't we all done things that, known or not at the time, were not going to turn out well? Even when we were told, warned and cautioned, we had to find out the hard way. We try wild new things; some kill us while others save many lives. Some get us praise and money, others leave us in bad health and friendless. Life is a comparative study. It's called trial and ERROR; we learn from mistakes. That alcoholic father wasn't a sinner or a loser, rather a man not yet done experimenting with how to find happiness. Some are slow learners: no judgment, just fact.

Is there a less painful and time-consuming way to learn than falling down? If you somehow "had a feeling this was not going to go well," you could make a different choice. That feeling is Guilt: it's nature's better way to teach you lessons, in advance, no messy clean-up. When used proactively, by listening to those queasy feelings and obeying them, it can save a lot of trouble. Beyond avoiding wrong, Guilt can guide you to act true to your own nature, be your best self and show you how to be proud of what you have done. It can clarify conflicting thoughts so you always know what to do and stand firmly behind your words and actions.

Listen to YOU!

The most essential part of this approach to working with Guilt is to separate the cloud of external influences—including the thoughts and beliefs in your head—from the truth in your heart. Do I mean all the rules parents and society taught you? Yes! The radical idea here is that when you are truly connected to inner wisdom, you know what is best and know any consequences are also for the best. The practice is the equivalent of going into a sound-proof, signal-free safe room so that the only voice is your own consciousness, intuition, heart, soul, or voice of God as you may imagine it. The aura shield meditation in the Anger chapter is a good way to create this. A shorter version of this essential step is included in the practice below.

///

Use Guilt to Guide From the Heart

Create a meditative environment inside and out. Spend several minutes breathing deeply and slowly, practicing mindfulness until you feel present, calm and fully aware of yourself.

Focus on your heart-center inside the middle of your chest. Take your stand here to defend your truest self and send away all other voices, people, thoughts and external influences. For now, only the purity of heart and soul will have a voice in this exercise, free of inner and outer critics and judgments.

Evoke compassionate understanding to remember any guilt-provoking event in your life. Whether intentional or a mistake you made unawares, there was a backlash that you felt bad about.

Review the scenario beginning to end without judgment or comment, neutrally. Be generous, kind and caring. Allow and observe all physical feelings and emotional energies to flourish without resistance, just breathe and remain steady and grounded in your body until you feel you can handle them. Get to an equilibrium between the visiting feelings and your stable sense of self that is stronger and greater.

Now you can observe, ask questions that your body and the feelings will answer. What did you do? What feelings and thoughts did you have beforehand and during? Listen to them now. Did you not hear cautions, or heard and ignored or overrode them? What was the motivation or reason to do the thing? Review all the many consequences. What suffering resulted? How did you feel about it all?

Breathe deeply and stay connected to your body and heart center. Keep a kind and compassionate view of your earlier self. Accept yourself as human, innocent and imperfect. From here you can see what at the time you didn't yet know, what you couldn't do, lessons you hadn't yet learned.

Knowing what you do now, how would you do the whole thing over again? See several alternatives you might have taken if you only knew. Imagine re-doing the whole scenario differently with what you learned.

Does that feel better? Does this give you a new personal directive for how to live?

> *"I cheated on my now ex-partner. I felt guilty for a long time after breaking up. It was hurtful to everyone involved. I was angry at and disliked myself for doing it. I now see how unhappy I was with my ex but didn't know how to speak up to break up or make it better. I didn't want to hurt him, so I sneaked instead. Now I am strong and communicate often with my husband so I don't feel frustrated and dissatisfied. I can forgive myself for that time; I did the best I could. I learned from that pain, it's better to speak up about problems so I needn't lie."* —B.K.

> *"I got into a bad situation with a colleague when we were intoxicated. I felt guilty and then angry for not listening to myself. I need to forgive myself. I now know how to listen to my instincts to ensure this doesn't happen again. I can trust and protect myself better now."* — Randi

Teaching or Venting?

Meditating on Guilt, a client learned a valuable lesson by connecting three events. Her father smacked her when she didn't give back an item she took after he told her to. She sees now that he hit her not for taking the thing, but out of his personal stress and his anger for not obeying him. Recently, her manager sent her searing emails over an error on a project that was beyond her previous experience. She realized she was being punished for having been assigned the plum project over her manager. And the day before, she had ripped into her son for throwing a rock at her. Her marriage was in trouble. In all three, she saw that the "punishment didn't fit the crime." Each authority was in a position to help the "wrong-doer" learn something from the incident, but instead was venting their anger. She remembered how it felt to be spanked for an innocent mistake and went to her son to talk calmly about rock throwing and how he might feel if he hurt someone accidently out of anger. Maybe she won't pass on the unfair harm done to her. Can you see the difference and move from punishing to teaching and learning?

Victim Blaming—Who's Fault Is Trauma?

Traumatic events write a big piece of our stories. Not only the event and its memories, but all that we come to believe about ourselves and the world in order to make sense of the chaos it creates. When tragedy hits, we want to know why it happened. The mind seeks to explain it and make a plan to hopefully avoid it from happening again. Was the accident my fault or theirs? It feels better to think I didn't cause this, so we jump to blame the other driver, the car, the weather, bad luck, or God. In the trial for the murder of Harvey Milk in San Francisco, the defense said junk food and sugar made the accused not responsible for his actions - the Twinkie Defense - and it largely worked! Blame hopes to avoid consequences like fines, jail, losing a job or relationship and to avoid feeling that we are bad for doing wrong. We blame to deflect taking responsibility: it's your fault that I am unhappy.

More often and especially in childhood trauma, we take on what is not ours. When we are young, it is crushing to imagine that the caregivers we depend upon are wrong; we blame ourselves for our parents' problems. That false narrative is supported by blamers and shamers. It's a rare child that can stand against the lie of self-blame when it comes from those in control. If I accept the story that everything is my fault, I will carry that lie with me into adulthood, into victimhood. Battered wives blaming themselves, sexual abuse victims hearing it was what they were wearing, if only I had known how depressed she was I could have saved her.

When the mind repeats the stories that trauma creates, it keeps the trauma alive. The troubled mind is desperately trying to find a way out but we are re-traumatized by the churning thoughts. Guilt (and Shame) can lock us into the old story through the lies we believed. These emotions can also be used to free us. The stories of Guilt and blame are based on a judgment that is handed down and accepted as the truth. But there are re-trials with new judges that result in reversals from guilty to innocent. You can review a case any time, use new information, reach a new conclusion and tell your fair accounting of the tale. No one wants to suffer, no one deserves to suffer, you are not to blame.

No-Fault Trauma—Taking Responsibility Gives You Control of the Narrative

No-fault insurance is a policy under which you are covered no matter what: the insurance company won't blame you so as not to pay. Blame is used to avoid taking responsibility and facing consequences. Taking responsibility for our actions, making amends and correcting future behavior are the remedies for guilt and a part of healing trauma. If you were blamed or blamed yourself, Guilt is there let you know if and when you have come out of an event clean and if not yet, what you need to do. Would you be willing to see traumatic events as earthquakes of human behavior? They happen. Whatever happens, no matter who caused it, you have to live with it. So only you have the right—and the responsibility—to choose how the story goes and how it ends. Did a disaster leave you living in the damage, or did it make you stronger and wiser?

Taking responsibility to clean up whatever mess we are left with is an empowered and healing attitude. Practice the previous exercise using a traumatic memory that you are comfortable with and ready to explore. Using your current consciousness, view the earlier version of yourself with great compassion to rewrite the story, your way. Try this mental exercise again and again as needed, to cleanse yourself of Guilt and blame. It takes effort to rewrite, but each time you go over the story in your mind and with each new day, make your story one of victory overcoming adversity, with lessons learned for a brighter future.

Using Your Better Judgment

You live within your story, so you get to be the one to tell it. Whether a past event or a decision you are trying to make, you are the judge. Can you be fair, compassionate about your history and dispassionate enough to avoid future fallout from your choices? Since the word judgment—"being judgey"—has a negative spin, we'll use its refined sister, discernment: "keenly selective judgment." Discernment requires cool emotions and a clear head; it requires a neutral position that does not take one side of the story over another. It's called the Neutral Mind, a pure and unbiased vision that calls on your highest values and virtues.

Knowing what is right, what to believe and what to do is not always easy. Lies are told convincingly, impassioned conspiracy theories have proof, fake news is confirmed by many. Apps can easily make videos of you saying and doing anything the user cares to create. Soon, robot avatars of you could commit crimes. We all need a more advanced system to find what is real and true; and we have it. We can be manipulated when others stoke strong emotions to have us betray ourselves, because feelings overtake rational thought. But when you remain neutral, you know what's true. The training for that is, once again, our friends mindfulness and meditation. The practice of holding the mind steady, not pulled uncontrollably by a thousand conflicting thoughts, is the same skill needed to sift through conflicting voices, news and tweets. Here's a quick practice:

/ /

See the Truth

Pick a debate question with two sides. A personal decision with pros and cons about what to do, or the two sides of an impassioned societal or political issue about what is right. In the former, the two opposing stories are in your own head. In the latter, you are on one side and those you disagree with are on the other.

Sit still with your hands open on each thigh, palms facing up. Put one of these arguments on your right palm, the other on your left. Focus on one hand as you listen to its viewpoint, then listen to the other side. Go back and forth, giving each side equal time; make both convincingly true. Soften your stance a bit to see that both have valid truths; there isn't a right or wrong. See that this debate could go on forever, like a ping pong match, with each side holding tightly and fighting to convince.

Now focus on the center of your chest, midway between these two sides. This heart center will be the impartial mediator of this conflict. Breathe and become peaceful, quiet and soft. When you feel at ease, peacefully watch the debate without taking sides, like a parent compassionately watching their two children arguing over nothing. Enjoy the peaceful view above all the noise and fuss where you can see everything clearly. For a few moments, you no longer care about which side wins, you just want peace: that is the most valuable thing. When you feel free of any favoritism, ask your heart to show you a higher truth at play. Keep your mind quiet and just receive whatever comes to you. Be patient: as soon as you try, the window of neutrality is closed; more answers come with practice.

From neutral mind, things feel right in an effortless way, distinct from efforts to think, prove and win your ideas. These truths are peaceful, effortless and inspiring. You will find yourself knowing things you might read in wise books, or that you were told many times. But when it comes through your consciousness, there is no doubt. What comes is your higher truth. Others may not agree or like it, but you know.

> *"Since I was a young girl, my parents constantly told me when I was a good girl or a bad girl. In school there were so many judgments about what I wore, who I was with and then all the rules about me and boys that would make me a bad girl. As a woman, I'm still doing everything to try to be their good girl and always worrying what other parents think about my parenting choices. I'm stuck in my job because I don't want my boss and husband to disapprove of my leaving."—Sarina*

Trusting Truth

It is confusing and stressful to live without knowing your truth, what is right and what to do. You were born knowing what felt right and what didn't. This is not the same "right and wrong" concept from the beginning of this chapter. This is about a deep sense of knowing that you are in harmony with your essential self and in satisfying sync with the world around you. This knowingness—what is right for you—is not based on fleeting pressures. Rather, there is peace and confidence in yourself even when the consequences are hard to bear. You live without regrets. This inborn guidance is too often lost early on in favor of the conflicting influences we want to appease. Guilt tugs at the gut to bring us back.

When a trusted adult touches a child inappropriately, it is shocking and awful, but the child is told it is okay, not to tell anyone. Traumatically confusing, knowing what is right is sacrificed to survival. Knowing the truth of what feels right becomes, "I don't know what to do, what to think, what I need." How could a human, evolved and adapted for millions of years, not know? Inner guidance is always there, ready to be awakened and used. I have assisted and witnessed countless times, both from a well-timed question and in mindful self-awareness, a person realizing powerful truth that only moments before they thought they didn't know. I'm saying that your inner guidance and living in integrity—your being and your actions are integrated—is always yours to recover.

The recovery process stalls when "I don't know how to do it" is mistaken for "I don't know what to do." You must separate and solve these two steps in order: first know, then do.

When you don't know what to do and a debate rages in your head, don't try to decide. Put your effort into quieting the mind, getting to a peaceful neutral state. It may take a moment or a month, but when you find a mere moment of clarity, ask the question and wait to receive the answer as if your entire being is the ear through which you hear. You know the truth when you feel it and it feels so good!

Then, don't let the doubt that long ago robbed you of intuition take over. Recover trust in yourself. Hold onto what

236

you know you need to say and do, *then* take on the question, "How?" It's okay if that takes a while. Use intuition and intellect together, then risk the action. It takes time to trust yourself again, to trust your truth. Trust is gained by testing over time. Challenge yourself to find out what is best for you, then obey your own inner wisdom. Small steps that feel right will build your confidence. Be patient, the right thing is often harder in the short term and takes time to prove itself with positive long-tern outcomes. When you have a moment of clarity, the "aha" moment that comes in meditation, hearing words of truth from wise ones, or in a flash, commit to it. You will continually become more trusting of yourself.

The Truth about Trust

When you have been hurt or betrayed, trust is broken. You may think you can never trust anyone again. Fine, don't! Instead, trust yourself! That bond with yourself can be lost in the mildest of traumas but like any relationship, it can be repaired. Trying to trust is often a fruitless effort to make sure you or another always behaves the way you want them to: *"Can I trust you this time to stop drinking?"* Holding on to wishful thinking rather than learning from history what to expect, you are caught off guard and devastated when they do it all over again.

The old understanding of Trust—to put your expectations onto others to get what you need—always falls into disappointment, argument and what is seen as betrayal. If they do behave the way you want, but are going against their own truth, the conflict it creates in them will eventually cause the arrangement—and possibly the relationship—to fall apart. More often, they may agree to your demands just to get out of trouble or from the inability to know and speak their truth, but not intend or be able to behave by your rules. If either party is not coming from their Truth, then real Trust cannot be formed. Upgrade your concept and use of trust from: "I want to trust people to act the way I want them to, so I get what I need," to true trust: "I trust myself to handle whatever others do, which becomes predictable with experience."

Compassionate trust is an educated and realistic understanding that sounds something like this:

I trust that you want to quit drinking, that it is possible and that you are not always in control of that addiction and may fail again to keep your word. Knowing that, I must do what I need to do to take care of myself, not be naive and devastated again. I trust that I too am imperfect and mean well but sometimes make mistakes. I trust that when you are stressed you become grouchy. I trust that you will be kind again after that. I trust that I can handle myself when you are not your best, not take it personally nor allow your known issues to harm me.

Forgiveness

In the paradigm upgrade from "sin and punishment" to "injurious mistake to learn from," there is a clear process of healing and resolution.

> The event
> Unwanted effect
> Realization of the cause that led to the consequences
> Acceptance of responsibility and ability to affect better
>   outcome
> Correction and change of the behavior, including
> Making amends; mending the harm
> Forgiveness of self and other

When the cycle is complete, all involved may enjoy the resulting upgrade in their knowledge, wisdom and consciousness: lessons learned, values clarified, virtues found. Assuming responsibility, making amends and forgiveness must all be genuine and each may take quite some time to learn and achieve, but those skills and attitudes may be the Universe's purpose in the whole affair. Don't forgive others for their sake; do it for you, because holding on with Anger to your wounds affects you much more than it does them. Instead, channel Anger's power into personal protection from further harm. Do whatever repair work you need to clean up any mess you've made—make amends. And forgive yourself for any part you played and for having to go through it.

When these steps are genuinely complete, which might be instantaneous or take some time, you are at peace and can let it all go. It's an individual process that can't be coerced or faked, but so worth genuinely reaching. Don't think forgiving is allowing: it is never a pass to continue bad behavior. And using true trust from the lessons learned, you won't let yourself be hurt again.

Forgiveness of anyone else is a gift you give to yourself. You may be surprised to find love and respect for yourself and others involved, humble appreciation of human imperfection, pride in yourself, or gratitude for the hard-knock lessons and growth.

Cursing and Blessing

Forgiveness is a power you have, a blessing you can bestow. You also have the power to curse: cursing others for what they've done and cursing yourself, are part of the old Guilt system—payback, vengeance, getting even, making sure you get yours and they suffer too. These perpetuate rather than alleviate the negative effects of misdeeds. Cursing is not just a sorcerer's magic and blessing is not just the Pope's hand on your head. A curse is ill will, pain wished upon someone, social media shaming and gossip. Such thoughts and feelings

239

live in you and affect you much more than your target. Who have you been cursing and how do you do it?

Giving blessings uplifts you. A smile, a kind word or gesture of help, thinking about someone and sending them love. Having food to eat, sunshine and trees are some of the countless blessings that life gives you each day. Think about the many forms of blessings you have been given and that you give to others. Have some fun with this free and unlimited power you have to bless. The power is yours to use.

Returning to Innocence

Harmful events always shock us out of a simpler, more innocent perception of ourselves and the world around us. We realize we have to deal with a much harsher and more difficult life. And since it's simpler to blame ourselves, we feel bad, dirty, wrong. Guilt replaces innocence. The story we tell ourselves changes. It logically would describe just the event but more often we indict our entire being: Guilt moves from a temporary state to becoming our identity. As with Anger and every other emotion, it no longer visits temporarily to make a correction, it moves in to stay.

A Truer Story and Better Use of Guilt

Innocence is an organic trait inherent in all things. Water, fire, trees and you have a benign existence, each with unique expressed qualities. Fire and flood have no evil intent, they act as is their nature. Humans love and kill, that is our nature. There are consequences for each, but we never become evil. Likewise, we never lose innocence and we have a choice of which to dwell in. Your state of innocence is not based on your history, your last deed, or a tally of good and bad deeds. Redemption is a choice, a state of consciousness that is always available. Rules, laws and judgments are constructs of the mind. Innocence is a permanent quality of the heart. Bad is a thought, compassion is a feeling. Love and self-love are condition-less, unlimited and always available, anytime you go into and come from your heart. Innocence is available by simply relating to it.

Practice to Know Your Innocence

Sit comfortably and still, eyes closed and take ten slow, deep breaths to calm yourself, focusing on any sensations in your body. Observe your mind's activity and let the conversation in your head quiet down. Imagine that your mind, your center of awareness is slowly dropping down like an elevator from your head to your heart center. From here, focus on physical sensations, breath and feelings. Bring in an image of simple innocence: a puppy playing, a tree, whatever you imagine to be pure or unspoiled. Focus on the feelings that arise. They are in you, in your heart. At that moment that feeling is you, you are that. Sit and enjoy the feeling.

By connecting to this part of you often, you don't have to lose it when harm is done. Guilt wants to return you to innocence and innocence melts Guilt. When you make mistakes—and you will—returning to your inborn innocence will allow you to openly admit, accept consequences, do what you can to clear it up and move on the better and wiser for it.

To-do List for Guilt-work

- Clear old Guilt so there is no harmful residue from your history. Use Guilt in a project to clear up the past, refine your personal standards and live truer to them. Name an area in which this is needed and the specifics that are required.

- Move from blame or denial to responsibility. Retake your power to write the rest of the story.
- Make right anything that's bothering you. Come clean with yourself and others.
- When you are accused of anything, get to a neutral state of mind, then compare their story to your highest truth. If you are off, correct it.
- Use Guilt to quickly correct fresh mistakes so you learn and recover quickly.
- Use Guilt to know yourself and the values that are required for your peace.
- Become fluid with making amends and generous with forgiveness.

Recovery Story

"I remember at 5 years old how innocent and good I felt. When I happily told my mom, she said, 'Oh, no, we are all born in sin and go to hell unless...' I thought, 'Oh no, I've got this all wrong; I can't trust myself to know what's true.' From that day I listened to everyone else and it's been such hard work trying to please. Then I remembered recently doing what someone wanted that was against my integrity; I didn't like the choice I made. I felt guilt very strongly in my body, a real, internal feeling, different from the haze of subtle guilt I feel all the time. I realized I am really good with guilt, I do know what is right, I'm just listening to too many opinions. My guidance system is quite good; I can quit listening to all those

*stories and just trust myself. Finally, I'm back
to listening to Me."* —Ember

Conscious Guilt is an opportunity for honest self-review. When you make a mistake, Guilt illuminates a chance to review your behavior and find what works for you and what doesn't. You can then correct your behavior to prevent those undesirable consequences from happening again. A key to finding the truth in your heart is to distinguish it mindfully from all external influences, then try it out until you learn to trust that inner voice. In Guilt-work, painful consequences are the motivation to learn, living through the lessons are the price paid and positive outcomes are the reward.

Chapter 11

Salvage Self-Esteem:
Use Shame to Care for Yourself

You are a social animal. Your happiness and even your survival, depend on getting along with other people. Banishment from the cave meant death from cold and starvation. Being laughed at by the cool kids at school made you feel like you wanted to die. Humans have a highly developed ability to sense if we are accepted or rejected, to know where we stand with others and what it takes to fit in. This emotional sensor is called Shame. Like Guilt, it can be used by others to hurt and control you. You may hurt yourself with it, or learn how it polishes compassion and love yourself, no matter what others may think. It is the most disempowering emotion because, in Shame, you turn against yourself: you reject or even hate something about yourself. Yet this same self-worth detector is also meant to help you fully accept your uniqueness and be able to enjoy being you.

> *"During puberty, people started saying how 'big' I had grown. When I understood they were talking about my weight, I became self-conscious. I began to feel rejected, that they wanted me to be different than what I was. I took on their opinions, didn't feel pretty or slim enough. I remember my dad telling Mum not to wear pants because she looked too fat in them and him being embarrassed of me in front of his business associates. AND I WAS NOT EVEN*

FAT!! But weight became everything. I decided I wasn't good enough to be with a good guy, wear cute clothes or try to be pretty. I spent the next decades trying to behave perfectly, getting good grades, working extra hard and believing I didn't deserve what I really wanted. How did it go from my weight to settling and being unhappy? But taking a fresh look at myself, I see a solid, strong, healthy body-type that's perfect for the kind of active outdoor life I love."
—Sarina

Scan through your early memories: how were you treated? Did you have embarrassing moments when you were laughed at, called dumb, left out, didn't have or know the cool things, didn't fit in, or measure up? As a boy or girl, how did you compare to social norms for your sex? How were the people around you treated? One client said her father degraded her mother as fat and ugly and she realized she looked just like her mother. Did you have more intense abuse or neglect? How did you feel? Horrible, I know. But if you are willing to feel and consciously deal with it now, you can heal the wounds of self-esteem that those experiences create. You can reclaim your dignity, recreate your self-image and redefine the basis of your worth. As uncomfortable as it may be, it begins by clearly knowing your starting place, the formation of your self-esteem and how it has affected your life to date.

Shame's Roots and Its Reach

Beneath the veneer of our modern lives, there is the basic urge to survive and from that, many self-protective questions as we go out into the wide world. Do I have what it takes to make it? Is who I am going to work and be sufficient to survive and succeed out there? Will they like me? How do I compare? Am I smart enough to pass, attractive enough to find love? Am I loveable? Am I enough? We compare to compete. We evaluate ourselves and form an idea of our worth: it's called self-worth, a picture of ourselves called self-image. This belief system is merely a set of familiar thoughts. It can change over time but is always set early in life and can be difficult to upgrade. Self-worth ultimately influences our success and happiness because it is like an internal thermostat of what we believe we deserve and are capable of. When self-esteem is set low, we expect less; more successful and attractive people, opportunities and rewards are out of our league, so we don't ask or try; we settle for whatever matches our perceived level of deserving.

How is this belief system that defines our value and confines our choices formed? Initially, by how others treat us. Self-worth is a story we now tell ourselves but was initially said to us. If you were fortunate to be born into a clean home with loving attention that filled your needs, those environments were like a mirror in which you saw yourself worthy of all that. But likewise, when treated poorly, you concluded that was what you deserved. You were so sensitive and vulnerable, dependent on the kindness of these strange people and the world into which you were born. It doesn't take much neglect—a delayed feeding time when you felt empty and alone—to believe that the world is not a friendly place. At that fragile early edge of survival, you couldn't understand that someone cared but delayed. Instead, your mind was busy instinctively adapting to the challenges of the environment, drawing conclusions and creating coping strategies from that limited experience. To fear that the caregivers you rely on are defective would mean you are on your own. Instead, "something's wrong with me" is a disaster as well, but more limited in scale. "I'm defective" is the false core belief that

246

produces Shame and is in turn, perpetuated by Shame. It's cringe-worthy to contemplate the devastation and self-incrimination that come from severe abuse and neglect on a sensitive and fragile being. It's something few of us have avoided.

> *"I see how shame became habitual and part of me. It's as if we reject and discard parts of ourselves in moments of pressure, then like a cruel trickster, shame waltzes in and occupies that space. Instead of feeling the wholeness that is our birthright, we have this parasite that eats away at us, without even realizing it."* — E.P.

Trauma Creates Shame/Shame Is Traumatic

Shame is a response to how you have been treated. Being mistreated, getting hurt, is the very essence of traumatic experience. So, trauma—whether in the form of abuse, neglect, exclusion and even accidents and acts of nature—produces Shame. These experiences diminish self-confidence and self-esteem and do so proportionately to the intensity and duration of the harm. Everyone is somewhere on the trauma spectrum, so we are all dealing with Shame in some form. Here are some everyday experiences shared by students doing this work to let you know you are not alone.

> *"My friends made fun of me when I reached puberty before them, making me bad for having breasts and liking boys."*

> *"My neighbors had more money and nicer things; seemed happier."*

"My home was dirty and cluttered."

"My mother was bi-polar. She would excessively love me in a creepy way one minute and yell at me for being such a loser the next."

"I was the smallest boy in my class."

"My priest said sex was sinful but then showed me pornography."

"My father would rage at my mother when he got drunk."

"My family made fun of gay people."

"My teacher laughed whenever I got the easy answers wrong."

"We were in a car crash when I was six that killed my little brother; I saw him die."

"I've made mistakes that others see and punish me for."

"I stuttered. I was the new kid at school. I was the tall girl. The redhead. They called me weird, stupid, uncool, ugly, a slut, a wimp."

"I was punished for: being angry, speaking up, making mistakes, low grades, unfairly, for no reason at all, or I didn't understand why."

"My older cousin raped me."

Examine the Wounds to Help the Healing

While it can be disturbing to recall severe trauma, getting to the origins of self-image help bring the unconscious and invisible into plain sight and, ugly as it may be, you can then take control of the "who I am" story. Use discretion to answer the following questions to your comfort level. Take your time and do it your way. Know thyself! The process of self-reflection and healing takes time and may be part of other work you are doing with additional resources and support.

Begin this self-review practice in a quiet place and in a mindful headspace.

What are the most potent negative memories you have about how people treated you? Were the messages direct or implied? Who did they come from?

What were the specific qualities or characteristics by which people judged you? How did that feel at the time? How does it feel when you remember now?

Can you remember when you began to abandon your un-self-conscious innocence and the negative talk started coming from you? What were those thoughts in your head?

Was self-blame created or encouraged by others?

Were there religious rules, familial and culturally specific norms that you didn't fit into and by which people judged you?

Did abusers make their abuse your fault (victim blaming and shaming)?

Were these negative messages balanced by any positive memories of feeling safe and loved?

Which messages that you came to believe about yourself remain with you to this day? Can you identify self-criticism and negative self-talk that you do or have done?

For now, simply sit with these uncomfortable memories

and feelings. It is an essential step in emotional healing. Once you are in a relationship with the feelings, they can begin their self-worth repair work.

/ /

Self-Blaming and Self-Image

I remember my father "spanking" me—it's a polite name for getting hit. I knew I was out of line, but the intensity of his anger was disproportional. At five years old, I could see he was taking his frustrations out on me. Still, his wrath felt like hatred: I thought I must be really awful to be treated this way, that I "deserved" it. If he doesn't love me, it's because I am unlovable. Blaming oneself for abuse is common. The dynamics of the power imbalance between someone stronger or in a position of authority or respect and their junior or dependent increase the likelihood of the abused believing they deserved the abuse. With that comes the belief, "I don't deserve better, to be safe, to be respected, to be loved." There is a catch-22 with self-blame and self-worth that snowballs on itself. Lack of self-confidence increases self-blame, which decreases deservingness and self-worth, which reduces self-esteem. And these beliefs are self-fulfilling: too often, what we get is close to what we expect.

Self-Image Is Self-Perpetuating

Good and bad experiences shape the beliefs regarding who and what you are, what you deserve, what you can expect and what you will put up with. Trauma lowers the bar. Once formed, beliefs about yourself drive your behavior and create in-kind results. It is clear from studies on Adverse Childhood Experiences that the earlier in life and more intense the harm, the more lasting and negative the impact on our beliefs, expectations and quality of life (see the link for more about ACE in References). Mistreatment perpetuates itself long after the initial injury has passed; shame and self-blame attract and allow continued abuse. Why do other people have it better or worse than you? It's not always good fortune or bad karma. The high-born suffer and fall, the lowly rise and thrive. Beliefs create attitudes that give up easily or push through challenges: either way, you will subconsciously feel, "I got what I deserved." Can you put together a broad picture connecting your early life experiences and the results that have followed? Think about examples of how your self-image affects your results, what you think is possible, what you are willing to try and what is too much to expect. See the formation and effects of Shame and happily, Sarah finding her worth in this story.

Sarah Salvages Her Self-Worth

> *"After my mother died, when my father married my stepmother, who had five girls, all super-model gorgeous and affluent, I became Cinderella overnight. She bought lots of trendy clothes for them but never for me. I felt like the ugly one. Most of my father's and stepmother's attention and praise went to them, so I felt I was never good enough, no matter how hard I tried to please them and to be accepted by my stepsisters. But I was smart and a hard worker and to this day, I am an over-responsible over-achiever. That has served me well in my career, but I've never been treated well in intimate relationships. My second husband is an emotionally unavailable alcoholic, just like my first.*

Working with shame, I realized that early on not receiving love, I felt unworthy of love—and have continued not getting it. Working hard has been my way to try to earn a sense of worth, but I am exhausted. So, with Anger's help, I started setting boundaries with my husband around his drinking and about how he needs to treat me if he wants to be with me. After years of his making and breaking agreements, I realized I deserve better, so I made the decision to divorce and I feel so good. I will never again let anyone treat me poorly."
—Sarah

If looking at all of this is overwhelming, sad, or despairing, keep going. Shame comes like an ugly angel to nurse our self-worth wounds and teach self-compassion. Working with Shame is vital to recovering a healthy self-image lost in trauma. Continuing to see how it operates is part of the healing process. Listen to how Sarah's story progressed with Shame-work.

"As I dive deeper into shame, I am noticing that my striving and pleasing others are diminishing. I'm allowing a little more space and flow in life, not trying to push myself so hard. I just don't need to. I'm so surprised by how much of a boost my self-esteem has taken. All the E.L. work has been giving me so many insights, but it's in the shame that I find myself waking up, challenging my old stories and having the courage to see things in a different light. Today, at this moment, I finally feel proud to be me and I feel grateful for all I have and that is absolutely what I deserve." —Sarah

How Shame Shows Up

Having looked at how Shame begins and plays out, let's identify other specific behavioral markers. Shame makes you want to hide, to not be seen so that others won't see what you believe to be so awful so that they won't throw stones, words, or disapproving looks at you. Your beliefs of inadequacy come from your personal history. Self-loathing isn't always directed at your entire being. Shame is often more subtle and specific: disgust or embarrassment over specifics of one's appearance, intelligence, or abilities. "I hate my thighs," "I'm stupid at math," "I never sing; my voice is horrible," "I can't be seen with this grey hair." Self-worth and confidence can be situational and area-of-life specific. Some are confident and successful at work but shrink and go defenseless in relationships, or the reverse. You might be comfortable talking one-on-one, but at some number of people, you get tense and shut down. One part of your body is fine, but another is gross. High on the Shame spectrum, one feels wrong about everything they are and do. You live with you, 24/7 for your entire life. Why wouldn't you embrace every flaw and blemish as a treasured part of your precious life? It's called self-love. Catch yourself hating on yourself, however small the thing. Cursing it is not the best way to motivate improvement. And other things can't be changed, but can still be useful.

Coping Mechanisms

To cope and to cover, we hide in many ways: isolating, not risking or trying, underperforming, giving in, allowing mistreatment, expecting and settling for less than we want, repeated failures, suffering and self-sabotage in many forms that seem like "the world is against me." We create results that match what we feel we deserve. I am not indicting anyone's trouble; I'm inviting a more in-depth look into the effects of our self-image. Beliefs seem to seek evidence to validate themselves. Struggle and rejection give fresh evidence to confirm feelings of worthlessness. This helps explain the familiar pattern in people with sudden huge success like previously poor lotto winners, rock stars and even finding the love one always dreamed of, that their lives often implode. The gap between self-concept and circumstances doesn't feel right at the subconscious level; like a thermostat kicking on the air conditioner, life cools back down to an expected, "comfortable" level. Self-criticism, self-blame and all negative self-talk are self-perpetuating symptoms of low self-esteem. More severe effects include anorexia, self-cutting and other forms of self-loathing self-punishment. Depression and suicidal thoughts often follow when we believe we live in a world that doesn't want us.

Perfectionism, workaholism, over responsibility and self-neglected caretaking are higher-energy responses to these same beliefs. Perfectionism is a cover-up for "I'm not enough." It is horrible to think and feel that we are not good enough, that we are not worthy of acceptance and belonging, so we find clever ways to earn the love we don't feel we deserve. But you can never prove a subconscious belief wrong; you cannot outrun a fear of inadequacy; you can never be perfect. Without deeper self-inquiry and focused mental and somatic re-patterning, the beliefs and their coping strategies most often remain. Continue your self-discovery now.

Look for Signs of Shame

Which words in the last few pages struck a chord in you, sounded familiar, or helped you realize something? Identify any of thoughts, behaviors and beliefs about yourself that may stem from Shame. Ironically, Shame would have you judge yourself harshly, blame yourself and feel bad about it all. Do this differently as a compassionate inquiry to discover, learn and heal yourself.

Look at the general quality of effort and results throughout your history and today.

> Which attitudes encourage or resist taking risks and making choices?
> How do you feel about your accomplishments?
> Do you deflect compliments and feel embarrassed by praise?
> Do you give too much to others until resentful and exhausted?
> Do you always think about what others are thinking of you and try to please them?
> Do people, especially close family members and intimate partners, treat you poorly?
> Do you stand up for yourself when others are taking advantage of you?
> Do you think about what you want to say when you are hurt or want something, but don't speak up?
> Identify the triggers of your shame. What will you see, hear, or think about that makes you feel embarrassed, small, not as good as others?
> Are these triggers similar or related to earlier experiences?

Don't feel bad about all this. Use it to awaken your self-love!

Distinguishing Guilt from Shame

It can be challenging to separate Shame from Guilt, but it

is crucial to do so because their purpose and benefits are distinct. Guilt relates to things you do, which are limited in time and impact and can be corrected. Shame refers to being, who you are, your identity. When you are shamed for the color of your skin, you cannot change that; your believed defects are inescapable. The existential pain that your very being is wrong is no less when coming from a changeable quality such as weight or behavior. Once you self-identify as defective, not this and too much that, it seems unchangeable, a lifelong quality. When you are less than, flawed, unlovable for who and what you are, it can sap your will to live—it feels hopeless (see Chapter 9, Depression). While Shame cuts deeper than Guilt, the debilitating effects of both emotions can be used by others to weaken, control and dominate. People use them as weapons to put others down, so they feel better about themselves. By getting to know these debasing emotions and discovering their higher purpose, you become immune to the untruths of others and stand firm in your value. Again, the wisdom Sarah W. found:

Shame is the opposite of yoga. Shame is a rejection of the self, a separation. Through shame we create a distance that grows over time. We reject parts of ourselves that are not what ego wants to feel good. We collect shame along our path and as we go further we wonder why we do not feel whole. But when you continue to tear off parts of yourself, what is left? This despite the internal truth we all have deep down, that we simply are who we are.

Re-writing the Story

Shame and self-worth are stories, first told to us, then repeated to ourselves. Thankfully, stories can be re-written. Recovery from the residues of social shaming and traumatic abuse and neglect is entirely possible. You may get an insight here that propels you forward. The process continues in the steady raising of your self-view over several years. Commit to it now; recovering precious self-esteem can be the most life-changing personal growth project you will ever undertake. It involves taking control of the stories you tell yourself about yourself. It is ultimately about self-love. It seems that it would be natural and automatic to be our own best supporter through life, no matter what happens. Strangely, it is not. Instead, it's as if we are born into a confusing maze, confronted with confusing misinformation about who we need to be. Solving the puzzle of who you are and fully embracing it means you exit the maze and get to live freely, enjoying and fully employing every significant part of your unique and fragile being.

Refer again to our definition of trauma healing in Chapter 2. Looking at it through the window of Shame, we can specify, "Feeling love and acceptance now, which you didn't get then, will heal you." When you realize the needs—we all have to be included, approved of, connected and loved—it is quite humbling. We are fragile and vulnerable before the powerful influence of how others treat us. Being shamed is traumatizing and trauma is shame-inducing. Therefore, trauma and Shame feed each other in a self-perpetuating cycle. Shame has us feel undeserving and unable to receive the very love and connection that heals Shame. But you can break this Shame-deprivation cycle. Once you identify Shame, find and feed what you need that was prevented or taken from you by trauma and Shame. Take time to do that now.

Recall and review your work with Desire. You can mindfully discover qualities of experience you need to feel good, in this case, what you need to feel good about yourself. Meditatively recall an event of embarrassment, rejection, or any relational trauma. Identify the feelings of Shame or any others and breathe deeply to allow them to flow until you feel stable enough to continue. Feel in your depths what you needed so badly that was not there for you. Ask what could have been said or done to make it better for you.

Imagine receiving any form of kindness, compassion and love. Imagine that you felt it then—and feel it now. Such good feelings may seem inaccessible even now, even from yourself; this too is an effect of trauma that you are working to remedy. How will you get those needs filled now? There are infinite sources of compassion, kindness, acceptance and love. These are among the many forms of our human love-and-connection needs. Determine how you can go about bathing yourself abundantly with them in your life today. Among the many sources, you are the best, most reliable and most important. Learning to be generous to yourself with these qualities is essential to healing the past.

/ /

Be and Let It Be

Rejection is a critical Shame-producing condition, so its opposite—acceptance—is an essential factor in healing Shame. It would be lovely if others did this for you, but the moods and actions of others are unreliable at best. Worse, if you don't believe you are worthy, no one can convince you; their kindness won't change your beliefs until you think you are worthy. I've seen too many people leave loving partners, believing they did not love them. Self-esteem is an inside job! You can and must do this for yourself.

I'm not asking you to love your faults right away: you may need to warm up to that. Acceptance does not require loving. Acceptance means to receive, as you do a letter that may have bad news, but you take it and read it all the same. Acceptance means to come to terms with, to deal with, to work with rather than against reality. Whether you love it or not, don't deny or reject it. Your wrinkles need love too! Welcome parts of yourself, as a hospital accepts a sick patient, offering healing treatments not dependent on any judgment of their value in the world. You are who you are; it takes a lot more effort to deny and refuse what is than it does to allow and then deal with reality. Anyway, "reality" is subjective, so don't believe everything you think! Instead, sort through your thoughts and filter out those that take you down.

In my case, it took a while to figure out why I pushed myself so hard to take on work and get things done to the point of total exhaustion. Despite all evidence evident to others, I felt incapable, a particular form of inadequacy that I couldn't handle things. So I regularly took on way too much in a desperate attempt to prove my worth by showing I could do a task or project. But there are only so many hours in the day (I slept only four hours so I could get more done) and true to my negative belief I just couldn't do it all.

After hitting a wall—my body couldn't run the race anymore—I decided to address just one of my many incapacities and faults: being on time. I was always late and always beat myself up about it. No system worked to be on time and I tried them all. My last-ditch effort was to give up (a horrible concept) and accept that I just wasn't able to do it (my worst fear). To admit that, yes, sometimes I just can't do things was painful. A request came to take on a new community project. To say, "I can't," felt like I would die, that everyone would hate me. But I didn't and they didn't—they were disappointed but then asked someone else.

I later calculated that one "no" saved me about 400 hours over the next year. Once I accepted that I couldn't do everything I was free not to have to take more on. Over time I became able to do the things that were important to me and reduced my workload to a manageable level; I seemed to become capable of my workload. Resentment and exhaustion vanished, for the price of some fleeting feelings of accepting my inadequacy.

///

Behold and Be Whole

What have you rejected and how will you embrace and accept it so you can be whole?

Name that part or aspect of yourself that was rejected. That rejection first came from an outside message, but only caused harm when you agreed and rejected it yourself. It is important to name what was denied. Was it physical aspects of your body, individual behaviors, skills and abilities, or qualities and personality characteristics? What did you come to believe was wrong with you, defective, too much, or too little? What made you different, weird, unlikeable, that couldn't be changed and concealed from the world? It can be extremely uncomfortable to face this—you may have felt better to hide it from yourself—but you are not whole without it. Your left arm may be clumsier than your right, but you need that arm, too!

///

> *"I've been in hiding. I need to shake off other people's images of me and reject people telling me who I am or what I am not. I want to find out for myself, learn who I am and begin to feel my essence again. Here are my mantras:*
>
> *Just try and trust that I don't need to be any different than the 'me' I am right now.*
> *I am strong and capable of so much more.*
> *It's ok to be the relaxed me, too.*

If others don't like it, that is ok.
Be gentle with myself.
Exalt myself—talk positively about myself.
Be with positive people. Go where there is
love."—Marina

Don't Be Mean to Yourself

Kindness is another step to heal Shame. Again, I am asking
for much less than self-love here. Just start being kinder to
yourself. That begins with noticing the ways you are mean to
yourself in bad habits, suffering and lack of self-care, critical
in your self-talk, harsh in self-judgment, lacking in healthy
boundaries. Do you say or do things about or to yourself that
you wouldn't say or do to a friend or a child? Are you mean,
abusive, neglectful? See your patterns of pain as just that,
being mean to yourself. We sometimes carry on or continue to
allow the messages and treatments we experienced as a child.
Recognize and stop that unnecessary nuisance. Treat yourself
better whether you feel you deserve better or not; break the
habit. Your psyche will slowly conclude that you are worth this
better treatment, which will, in turn, make kindness come
more naturally. I am amazed by how often clients do this kind
of work and find others treating them better without saying a
word about it (but don't hesitate to set boundaries and
stronger requirements). Be nicer. Compassion will help with
that.

Compassion Helps

Kindness may be asking a lot from yourself when you
don't feel deserving of it. There are ways to crack open a cold
heart because your heart never turned against you; that was
all in the mind. Compassion is passion that comes from

identifying with the object of your compassion, so self-compassion should come first and most natural. Here again, you don't yet have to love or approve of some alienated part of yourself to have compassion. If you need to start with sympathy, go ahead; feeling sorry for yourself is the start of a detectable heartbeat, but is too close to apathy to stay there for long. Upgrade to compassion soon. Following is a practice adapted from *The Tibetan Book of Living and Dying*. It was so helpful when I read Sogyal Rimpoche giving instructions for working with a dying person. He says that one needs compassion to be with the dying, but you may not feel it. It is beautifully compassionate to accept that one might not feel what they "should."

Close your eyes and take a few deep breaths. Think back to any time at all when you felt warmth in your heart, a memory of any kindness you gave or received. A smile or word, the sun, or peaceful moment of contentment, gratitude, or hope. Search for anything that can stir a bit of positive energy akin to loving-kindness. Like a spark, focus on that feeling and nurture it to become a warmer flame. It is in you and can be for you. Send that feeling to yourself and, in turn, receive it. Like starting a campfire in the dark woods, it can take time and patience to get it going. With practice, it will be strong enough to warm you against any pressure from the outside.

Just as a relationship grows with time and becomes stronger through good times and challenges, a friendship with yourself can deepen into self-love. Begin to see this as the more natural state of your existence; from here, self-loathing is a distant oddity. The most important relationship in your life is the one with yourself. Spend the time it takes to "make up" and become good friends with yourself. Develop trust in and loyalty to yourself. When you make mistakes, are criticized or betrayed, don't abandon your one faithful and lifelong companion. Any great relationship requires attention and investment; take time to know, appreciate and come to love yourself.

Stable Self-Esteem

Countless times every day we face internal and external scrutiny, evaluating ourselves: "Am I worth it? What is my worth?" The automatic answer from the subconscious will be based on our history, primarily from early childhood experiences and outside influences. Our attempts to improve our worth can come by way of personal efforts to do more, do better, improve our performance, please others and work for their approval. If all goes well and public opinion goes in your favor, self-esteem gets a boost. But as soon as someone has a negative vote, you can as quickly feel deflated. While we start in life with a self-image created by and dependent on external validation, we must eventually find a firmer basis, or the ups and downs never end. Any basis of self-worth that is physical (appearance), temporary (our best or last achievement) and finite (human capacity) is at best a slippery and unstable foundation. Anything high today can be low tomorrow: the stock market, opinion polls, celebrities, fads, fashions, how many likes and followers one has, what goes viral is soon forgotten, friends fade and fortunes change.

If there were something unlimited that does not change, it would be a stable bedrock of self-worth. That must be something non-physical, timeless, ageless and enduring. A flower is beautiful and will die, but beauty itself is a virtue that is ever-present. And as a non-physical quality or essence, it is unlimited; there are infinite amounts available anywhere, any time. Physical strength may wax and wane in your body, but the qualities of timeless strength will always be part of the Universe and there to call on. In what ways are you strong and beautiful, qualities that are intrinsic to you as a human being, neither earned, achieved, nor exhausted over time? We are all things at once: beauty and ugliness, strength and weakness, a combination of opposites in constant movement. When you focus and call upon your empowering virtues, you manifest and enjoy them even while their opposites are also there. When you sing the story of your positive qualities, they are available and will be seen by others. This way, you can take back control of your story; you define yourself.

I have never met with a person who was not able to, even in times of low confidence and high Shame, name a positive personal characteristic. "I have never been treated well by any man, but I know I am a kind person." If that person has lived with great Shame, but can acknowledge and live with the power of kindness, they can feel good, proud and be happy. One virtue, unflinchingly self-validated, is enough to raise your self-esteem. Owning your kindness doesn't require that you are always kind; instead, you are all things and choose to define yourself by kindness, regardless that you will also be unkind at times. Your meanness is not a failure that demeans you when it is recognized and also accepted as part of you. Temporary states only define you as human; acceptance of light and dark sides is liberation from Shame and its ultimate lesson. You are free to be you.

Watch a baby exploring or a child playing. We remember that carefree state of simply being. And we experience that when fully engaged in something; we simply do it without self-conscious checking on ourselves or judging. All lives begin with innocence and move through the hard-knocks that challenge it and thus weaken the connection to that pure and simple self. Each of us can return to that precious home in which we again know and love ourselves. Perhaps this is what Jesus meant by: Unless you become as little children, you cannot enter heaven. What were the qualities born with you? Who were you before you tried to be something? What do you value and can be appreciated for without effort?

See Yourself More Deeply

When you look in a mirror, what do you look at and what do you look for? At your face for blemishes, at your skin for signs of aging, at specific body parts for sexiness, at your muscles for impressive size, at your clothes for in-style-ness? How do you measure up; how do you like what you see? What if what you see in the mirror was your goodness, your humble courage, or your sincerity of purpose? Make a list of five qualities, character values and virtues that you know you have, like about yourself, or even aspire to and want to bring out. (If you are stumped, search the Internet for a list of virtues and reacquaint yourself with the stuff that older civilizations praised and aspired to.) Look in the mirror and while checking to see if your hair is straight and no food is showing in your teeth, see, admire and enjoy those qualities. Practice walking around feeling good and proud of these aspects of yourself as your peacock feathers.

Using Shame for Self-Improvement

In addition to being wrongly shamed, we sometimes act in ways that are beneath our standards. We express both light and dark sides as a way of learning which to follow. In the end, it is the light that we most enjoy. Consciously applied Shame is a tool to review, assess and align ourselves to that highest version of self, which we most enjoy. When Shame shows up, it is time to check if we are being true to ourselves; this is its highest purpose. Skillfully applied Shame has three keys:

1. Mindfulness—a neutral state of mind for accurate

discernment

2. Ability to separate outside criticism from an internal assessment

3. Willingness to see, accept and correct self-determined flaws

Whenever negative judgment comes at you, whether from a person, the media, or your thoughts, imagine it coming at you like an arrow in slow motion. If it penetrates—you accept and agree with that judgment—it will wound and weaken. Stop the arrow at least nine feet from your body. If you already feel hurt, upset, or angry about it, you will need to come back and do this later when you feel neutral and non-reactive. When you can be in a state of clarity, examine the message carried by that freeze-framed arrow. Scrutinize the source of the message: what are the conditions and the motives? Is there any truth at all to the message? Or is it purely their agenda having little to do with you, their current target? Is there any bit of useful truth in it, something that helps you see yourself from another angle, something you could take in and learn from and upgrade to your better self? If so, keep that and make some changes while discarding the rest. Use feedback but only after filtering through your neutral mind and desire to be your best self.

A Better Recipe for Self-Esteem

We typically depend on a mixture of self-esteem sources composed of roughly:

- 70–85% external validation, approval of physical characteristics, changing conditions
- 10–25% internally generated and self-acknowledged qualities

- 0–5% universal and intrinsic, existential and inborn attributes we share with all things

Imagine your life and this world if we all inverted that formula. What if the competition, the marketing ads and peer pressure were all about the higher human qualities, our angelic nature?

- 60% universal qualities, virtues and higher values; the truths about yourself that are beyond time and space, beyond success and failure: truth, dignity, nobility, love...
- 30% internal validation. Here you identify and live by what you hear from your heart and soul.
- 10% external feedback. This keeps you in sync and flow with others, prevents getting lost in arrogance and ego: a reality check.

You can make and live by your own internally realized recipe for self-esteem. Rather than pursuing an unending wish list of things to have and do to feel good about yourself, meditate on the beauty of existing, the miracle of simply being as you are. This is the highest psycho-spiritual work any of us can do.

Conclusion

We All Want to Feel Good

If you have made it this far with me, your relationship with emotions has changed for the better, forever. If you have practiced all the exercises, you now have direct personal experience with the benefits of befriending your feelings. And if you skipped them, I urge you to go through them now because you can't recover mental health through mentation alone. Like a song's refrain, re-read right now the first few pages of this book to realize how much you understand about your emotions and self-therapy. You've seen that time spent willingly feeling your "bad" emotions leads you to feeling better, because they carry instinctive and intuitive answers. From here, I leave you to a lifetime of further discovery and growth with some thoughts on happiness.

Let's assume that everyone is doing the best they can to be happy. If so, why aren't we better at it? Perhaps the pursuit of happiness—which the US Constitution claims is our right—is not the right goal. Not that it isn't achievable, but that as a goal it has sent us on a fruitless path: pushing to achieve uninterrupted pleasure we believe we are entitled to, while thinking discomfort means something is wrong. Here's an approach better aligned with how the world actually works: life is a constant dance of opposites—day and night, winter and summer, birth and death, pleasure and pain. Feeling up and feeling down *is* life. Accepting it all, moving with, learning and growing from what life brings with humility and gratitude, these are goals we can achieve and this has been our approach.

Our fundamental shift is to rethink "negative" emotions as

protective and "positive" emotions as flourishing and that there are times to protect and times to flourish. I hope you no longer consider the seven emotions examined here to be negative at all. Protective emotions arise spontaneously, as needed. In some cases, we invite them—we go for the thrill of an amusement park ride or the rush of a horror movie to feel the excitement of Fear—but we mostly don't want or seek them out. Whether we like these feelings or not, we need them and can master the skills that help them to do their jobs. Emotional liberation embraces the fact that we all experience darkness: abuse, neglect, heartbreak, rejection, scarcity, loss and the troubling thoughts and feelings that always follow. And when we accept them, face and embrace what we'd rather avoid, we are made whole. Living with all that you are, whether judged as good or bad, happy or sad is, well, a happy life. Your best self is your entire self, warts and all! You feel good when you face whatever feels bad.

Flourishing is Your Natural State

Things harmful to your well-being summon protective emotions and energies. When you use them to resolve the harm and get what you need, you feel relieved, more positive. That experience leads us to conclude that flourishing emotions arise naturally when nothing disturbs you; flourishing is our default state of being. Watch a baby sleeping or looking quietly and wide-eyed at the world. She seems peaceful until she is hungry, cold, or tired. Just like you, she cries until that need is satisfied, after which she returns to contentment. That feeling good is normal, while negative feelings are a temporary interruption, will seem counter-intuitive to those who have spent much of their life removed from good-feeling experiences due to trauma. But as we clear our past and elevate ourselves beyond the effects of harm, this paradigm—

that flourishing is natural—becomes evident. Hope, beauty, gratitude and their like are always there whenever there is nothing detrimental to block your ability to feel them. Rather than pursuing happiness, expect it as a natural outcome of handling the obstacles before you. Further, happiness need not be fragile and dependent on good feelings alone. Fluid changes of up and down energies and moods are as natural as the weather: each condition is equally precious. There's a story that the Dalai Lama was asked if he ever got Angry. He laughed and replied, "Yes, but I recover quickly!" He speaks of an ability to move fluidly between emotions—high and low—as needed, without getting stuck, to recover and return to a baseline of well-being.

Trying to Feel Good

In addition to enjoying our flourishing emotions by removing obstacles, we can intentionally create them. Isn't this what we spend most of our time trying to do? Physical pleasures are our primary go-to for trying to feel good, but the feelings don't last long and require constant repetition. It's not that we shouldn't seek pleasure, but we must also recognize and remove sources of pain—toxic relationships, destructive habits, poor self-care and weak boundaries—rather than cover them with temporary enjoyments. Protective emotions alert you to these obstacles to happiness, but you must do the work to correct these conditions and live beyond struggle and stress.

Better self-care starts with taking responsibility for and learning what you need to function at your best. Cultural messages to compare, compete and work hard on the one hand, but indulge ourselves in food and luxuries on the other, are conflicting pressures that keep us running for but not reaching fulfillment. Only you can know, by your own comparative study, what brings you happiness. It takes honest, patient introspection to understand your path and courage to walk on it in your way. In this, life is like the game we played as kids to find a hidden treasure, given the clue "colder" when we moved further from it and "warmer" as we got close. In time, you can find the things that bring you good feelings. There are many ways to stimulate flourishing emotions, do everything you can to raise your mood and prevail over negativity.

"The world is so full of a number of things, I'm sure we should all be as happy as kings." —Robert Louis Stevenson

But seeking good things alone as a road to happiness can be used in denial of real issues that one needs to address. Attempting to feel good can be used to cover up pain that wants to be healed, like make-up on a sickly face. When we use pleasure-seeking to desperately cover suffering, it becomes overused and under-performing; distractions become addictions. I began working with the protective emotions after observing denial hidden in the pursuit of good feelings, both in popular culture and in the self-improvement and spiritual communities. I found workshops for heavy emotions much less popular than those promising beautiful feelings. This book serves to reach a balance between the overused path of trying to feel good with the underused need to be real about our dark side by digging into big issues and their feelings to get back to living light.

The Study of Happiness

We know happiness when we feel it. Can we define it? Can science help us achieve it? Psychology and psychiatry have been primarily working in a disease-based model of mind and emotion with a focus on mental illness. Thankfully, the newer field of positive psychology looks at happiness, what it is and how it can be achieved. In the words of Martin Seligman, credited as its founder, "Positive psychology is the scientific study of optimal human functioning [that] aims to discover and promote the factors that allow individuals and communities to thrive." This definition implies that optimal human functioning includes happiness but has a broader scope and more moving parts we can use. This field names three related areas that make a positive, good, or happy life: the subjective, individual and collective. As you read them, evaluate how they are going for you. They might give you some ideas for ways to upgrade your life.

The subjective level is the inner world of your own feelings. Yes, scientists now study positive experiences such as satisfaction, joy, contentment and happiness. The individual level examines the human virtues and strengths that predictably produce a good life by studying hope, courage, determination, love and the many skills needed to be productive and get along with others. The group level of positive psychology focuses on what is required for us all to get along as a society: tolerance, altruism, ethics and good citizenship.

Positive psychology researcher Dr. Ilona Boniwell defines happiness in two parts. The first is mental, what you think and believe. Are you satisfied with what you have, who you are and what you have done in your life? It's how you feel when you compare yourself to others and to your own expectations. The second part is emotional: positive affect. Happiness is positive feelings and emotions, felt more often in proportion to the unhappiness of negative feelings and emotions. She acknowledges that we need to feel both, but the more positive feelings we live with as compared to the negative ones increases our perceived happiness.

In one study of the subjective level, Dr. Boniwell asked people in Britain how they define happiness and found five most reported topics. Seventy percent defined happiness by the love they feel in relationships with others. Fifty percent said happiness depends on peace with themselves: contentment with what they have and who they are. The third most important determinant of happiness was good health and security. Fourth was fulfillment in work: liking and being engaged in what they do. The fifth most reported source was a meaningful life, making a contribution to the world. These self-reported sources of happiness closely follow Maslow's hierarchy of needs and confirm our work with Desire as our guide to satisfying needs. It seems that happiness is about getting what you need to be happy! What do you need?

Beyond Positive and Negative

We have reframed the game: to feel and deal with the dark side and pursue the light of our human needs while accepting both equally. To take control of your happiness, you can use negative emotions for their positive purpose and you can generate positive thoughts and feelings. Is there an end to this dizzying dance of opposite qualities, this ping pong game no one wins? A solution comes with neutrality. As discussed in Chapter 3, the mind can observe and remain calm through good and bad. Think of any pair of opposites as the bottom corners of a triangle: neutral is the top of that triangle. Above and connected, it sees both without taking sides. From that vantage point, you are neither overtaken by emotion nor blocking it by the power of intellect. You are aware and open to all that is. Only when you don't take a side can you see all sides and only then can you see the right way to go and only then do you truly have the freedom to choose. To our detriment, neutrality is not widely used, but everyone can develop it. There are many ways to develop neutrality, but they all take practice, build awareness through self-reflection and involve learning to control the urges of the body and impulses of the mind.

Neutrality gives you the ability to keep your head clear in any situation without reacting. Neutrality is functionally the opposite of emotionality. You can be in the presence of others' strong emotions without taking them on. When you are comfortable with your own emotions and understand how to process them, it gives you the power to see what's going on when others are emotional; you let them have their emotions without unwillingly joining them in those emotions. Neutrality gives you emotional skill and emotional skill helps you remain neutral. This does not make you unfeeling and numb. It is emotional liberation, the freedom to choose what you do with feelings.

Taking full responsibility for your feelings, you no longer feel responsible for the feelings of others by blaming yourself or accepting their blame. When someone is feeling emotional, you are able to feel what they feel, but can differentiate your feelings from theirs. You use your skills to take care of yourself first. You don't have to fix people, but rather have the necessary distance to effectively help them when you choose to do so. You don't jump in the water to save them; you can throw them a lifeline.

Your Peace Leads to World Peace

As your inner conflicts diminish, so do your conflicts with the world around you. It is natural to want to pay happiness forward. I hope you will continue increasing your well-being and share what you learn about how to do so. But know that your happiness is in itself a real contribution to world peace. To be emotionally liberated is to effectively handle life's many joys and challenges, fully present and able to move through whatever comes your way. You feel what you need to be feeling whenever you need to feel it, for as long as it is needed, to know what you need to know and take care of yourself. You learn from the past without being stuck in that non-reality. You learn from each experience as a comparative study to continue growing more empowered, wise and peaceful—until and including your last day. This is not the end of your healing work, but rather a fresh start with new tools. Continue your journey to full recovery, a life richly textured with feelings, to emotional liberation.

References: Notes and Works Cited

Introduction

Roger T. Mulder, *Perspectives in Biology and Medicine*, Johns Hopkins University Press, Volume 51, Number 2, Spring 2008, pp. 238-250.

Metabolism Journal, Madhu Kalia, Volume 51, Issue 6, Part B, June 2002, Pages 49-53.

Chapter 1

Chapman, Gary. *The Five Love Languages: The Secret to Love That Lasts*. Chicago, Northfield Publishing, 2015.

Dynamic Equilibrium concept: Levine, Peter A. *In An Unspoken Voice, How the Body Releases Trauma and Restores Goodness*. Berkley, North Atlantic Books, 2010.

Rosenberg, Marshall B. *Nonviolent Communication, A Language of Love*. Encinitas, Puddle Dancer Press, 2005.

Chapter 2

More on Resilience: https://www.apa.org

For further discovery about Adverse Childhood Experiences, visit:

https://www.cdc.gov/violenceprevention/childabuseandnegl
ect/acestudy/about.html

For a deep dive into trauma, visit:

https://www.ncbi.nlm.nih.gov/books/NBK207191/

Levine, Peter A. *In An Unspoken Voice, How the Body Releases*

Trauma and Restores Goodness. Berkley, North Atlantic Books, 2010.

Maté, Garbor. *In the Realm of Hungry Ghosts, Close Encounters with Addiction.* Berkley, North Atlantic Books, 2010.

Shapiro, Francine. *Getting Past Your Past.* Rodale Press, 2012.

Van Der Kolk, Bessel. *The Body Keeps the Score.* Penguin Books, 2015.

Chapter 3

https://www.neuronation.com/science/benefits-of-smiling
https://alzheimersprevention.org/research/journal-articles/
https://pdfs.semanticscholar.org/a457/b65818faa4a88f65e4
d5e350b1f48395993e.pdf

Levine, Peter A. *In An Unspoken Voice, How the Body Releases Trauma and Restores Goodness.* Berkley, North Atlantic Books, 2010.

Maté, Garbor. *In the Realm of Hungry Ghosts, Close Encounters with Addiction.* Berkley, North Atlantic Books, 2010.

Van Der Kolk, Bessel. *The Body Keeps the Score.* Penguin Books, 2015.

Chapter 4

Dalai Lama, *Time Magazine Interview*, March 18, 2019

Khalsa, GuruMeher. *Senses of the Soul.* Kundalini Research Institute, 2013.

Emotions as algorithms. Yuval Noah Harari, *Homo Deus: A Brief History of Tomorrow* (New York: HarperCollins Publishers, 2017), pg. 83, etc.

Map of Consciousness available at
https://veritaspub.com/product/map-of-consciousness-
dr-david-hawkins)
Transcending the Levels of Consciousness, David R. Hawkins,
M.D., Ph.D., Veritas Publishing 2006.
Power vs. Force, David R. Hawkins, M.D., Ph.D., Hay House,
1995.

Chapter 6

By many measures it's the safest time to be a human on earth
(http://www.pri.org/stories/2014-10-23/world-actually-
safer-ever-and-heres-data-prove)
Why We're Living in an Age of Fear :
https://www.rollingstone.com/politics/politics-
features/why-were-living-in-the-age-of-fear-190818/
Anne Case and Angus Deaton (2017). "Mortality and Morbidity
in the 21st Century." *Brookings Papers on Economic
Activity.* Spring 2017. https://www.brookings.edu/wp-
content/uploads/2017/08/casetextsp17bpea.pdf.
From:
https://www.jec.senate.gov/public/index.cfm/republican
s/2019/9/long-term-trends-in-deaths-of-despair
"The Serenity Prayer" is the common name for a prayer by
Reinhold Niebuhr (1892–1971), made widely known by the
Alcoholics Anonymous organization.

Conclusion

Maslow, A. H. (1954). *Motivation and personality.* New York:
Harper and Row.
Dr. Ilona Boniwell, *Positive Psychology: Theory, Research and*

Applications (2011, Open University Press)
http://positivepsychology.org.uk
Mihaly Csikszentmihalyi, *Flow: The Psychology of Optimal Experience* (Harper Perennial Modern Classics) Paperback, July 1, 2008)
The Principles and Practice of Yoga in Health Care, by Dr. Sat Bir Khalsa, et al., a compendium of theory, research and practice of yoga and meditation for physical and mental therapeutic intervention.

About Atmosphere Press

Atmosphere Press is an independent, full-service publisher for excellent books in all genres and for all audiences. Learn more about what we do at atmospherepress.com.

We encourage you to check out some of Atmosphere's latest releases, which are available at Amazon.com and via order from your local bookstore:

Eat to Lead, nonfiction by Luci Gabel

Pandemic Aftermath: How Coronavirus Changed Global Society, nonfiction by Trond Undheim

Geometry of Fire, nonfiction by Paul Warmbier

Chasing the Dragon's Tail, nonfiction by Craig Fullerton

Great Spirit of Yosemite: The Story of Chief Tenaya, nonfiction by Paul Edmondson

My Cemetery Friends: A Garden of Encounters at Mount Saint Mary in Queens, New York, nonfiction and poetry by Vincent J. Tomeo

Change in 4D, nonfiction by Wendy Wickham

Disruption Games: How to Thrive on Serial Failure, nonfiction by Trond Undheim

Eyeless Mind, nonfiction by Stephanie Duesing

About GuruMeher Khalsa

GuruMeher means "teacher of compassion." His love of science and the desire to know how things work led him to study astrophysics at Cornell University. Depression and feelings of inadequacy shifted his interest to the Inner Universe - how we humans work and how that understanding can give people tools for happiness. Eastern philosophies and yoga for self-actualization, through a rigorously disciplined personal practice, became his crucible for self-healing.

Attracted by the idea of global change through personal transformation, teaching yoga and meditation became the way he could share what he found with others. He has trained thousands of yoga teachers internationally.

Through twenty years of counseling individuals and couples as a Professional Life Coach and Certified Yoga Therapist, he found that his clients could find answers to their problems with simple guidance and mindfulness techniques from yoga. Astounded by the predictable consistency of human emotional response to problems and trauma, GuruMeher theorized that each difficult emotion is a natural ally, awakened for a specific function to handle our challenges. His clinical work showed that to be true and resulted in the *Senses of the Soul method*, which has been called "the next evolution in therapy". It is based on the premise that emotions are not problems to be treated, but are analogous to our immune system's response to an infection; they are part of a remedy to heal difficult experiences. This mindful use of emotions has proven to be an effective path to self-healing, inner guidance and personal power.

GuruMeher holds a big vision for global peace through individual emotional health, which is accessible to everyone. He continues this work through online courses, workshops, teaching and counseling at www.sensesofthesoul.com.

Happily married for 35 years, GuruMeher and his wife, Siri Atma, live in Los Angeles, CA where they raised two emotionally strong children. They plan a return to their southern roots by building a home in the mountains near Asheville, NC.

GeorgHirschLifestyle

Alex

CPSIA information can be obtained
at www.ICGtesting.com
Printed in the USA
BVHW092143080322
630899BV00005B/733

9 781636 496061